'A strong and positi' ... d.'
Professor Dave L

CW00734839

EMPOWERING

HR

BUILDING THE VALUE AND STRENGTH OF HR

Deborah Wilkes

Empowering HR

First published in 2021 by

Panoma Press Ltd
48 St Vincent Drive, St Albans, Herts, AL1 5SJ, UK
info@panomapress.com
www.panomapress.com

Book layout by Neil Coe.

978-1-784529-30-7

The right of Deborah Wilkes to be identified as the author of this work has been asserted in accordance with sections 77 and 78 of the Copyright, Designs and Patents Act 1988.

A CIP catalogue record for this book is available from the British Library.

Dedication

For Paul

and for all the dedicated HR professionals out there

Acknowledgements

My first thanks go to Lisa Wyatt Sherman, who said one day, "You should write a book," and to Liz Priest, who then put me in touch with Mindy Gibbins-Klein, who made it all happen. More about Mindy later. Others who have been generous with their time and thoughts are John Dolton, Cherry Iley, Lorraine Green, Carl Kneeshaw and Robert Kelly. I am so grateful for your encouragement and support.

A book like this is the culmination of many years of learning from others, and with that in mind there are many others I would like to thank. My clients have provided a rich environment for learning; it is a privilege to work with chief executives and with talented human resources (HR) and learning and development (L&D) people and to be trusted with their projects and their people.

I must thank The Oxford Group for a wonderful associate relationship for 25 years, and in particular Nick Cowley, Nigel Purse and Gill Webb for their wisdom, talent and compassion, and for trusting me with fabulous as well as demanding clients.

I've enjoyed active membership of the Chartered Institute of Personnel and Development (CIPD) for many years and thank my professional body for providing opportunities to learn, connect and deepen relationships with HR professionals. Particular thanks go to Peter Cheese for transforming its relevance and building the credibility of the profession.

Thanks also go to Dave Ulrich for his immense contribution to HR over many years, and recently for his kind and generous engagement with my posts and his support and encouragement in the writing of this book.

I also want to thank George Naylor, my fellow founder and director of Enable-HR International, and friend and colleague for 30 years. George has a rare ability to get to the crux of reality in his surveys and brought that to our research, as well as the depth of his organisational understanding and commitment to people at work everywhere.

Finally, more about Mindy's amazing contribution as coach and publisher. She is inspiring as well as practical, and the writing process she shares enables you to write your best book. Thank you also to the team at Panoma Press for their wonderful support and for bringing this book into the world.

It's been an exciting and scary journey, and my husband and family have supported me all the way. My love and thanks, as always, go to them too.

Contents

Introduction

These are exciting times for human resources. There has never been a better time for HR leaders to take their seats as strategic drivers of business performance. Indisputable evidence now proves that the best organisations have the most dynamic human resources functions. However, HR professionals cannot succeed alone. They can deliver only when their work is embedded in the organisation, embraced and lived by its leaders and managers.

To deliver real value, HR must operate from a position of strength. Those HR leaders who can take on their chief executive and other business leaders and help them think more clearly are worth their weight in gold to their organisations. Their understanding of the business and of people wins them a hearing and leads to a powerful people agenda, which in turn improves business performance.

This robust partnership can then be created at every level between HR and the business. Whatever their level, HR people build on their professional platform of expertise with skilled challenge and by asking the right questions.

If you are an HR leader or professional, this book will help you build powerful relationships that deliver results. If you are a chief executive working with HR, you will see how to get more from your HR function.

Let's not pretend that this ideal is easy. Chief executives are surrounded by issues and want HR to clear them up. HR people have a myriad of governance, performance and management issues that weigh them down every day. There is a gravitational pull towards process and entrenchment. This book will help you to fight this reactive cycle – to create opportunities for HR to rise up and lead.

Now is the time. Huge changes in the world of work are building into a landslide. These unstoppable developments have urgent implications for how we organise work. This will demand collaboration of the most courageous, curious and generous kind between clever minds. Sharing expertise, insight, intuition and humanity has never been more vital. HR is at the fulcrum of this, but the ideas in this book apply to all.

Empowering HR is a two-way street

Let's start with some challenging questions for our key players.

First, for the chief executive:

What if I empowered HR to play its full strategic role? What if HR people were in the room with me every day, pushing me, helping me to think about my leadership as well as the business? What impact would that have on creating the best conditions for our people – and therefore our profitability?

Second, for the chief HR officer or HR director:

What if I empowered my chief executive to be the best leader they can be? What if I facilitated their thinking about people *and* business? What if I understood the business well enough to be seen as a future chief executive? What impact would that have on the influence of my HR function – and our ability to drive profitability?

Imagine if these questions were the starting point of a conversation between HR and the business at every level.

I use the terms 'HR and the business' and 'business leaders' throughout this book to draw an important distinction between HR leaders and those not in HR. I don't mean that HR leaders aren't in the business. They are.

Similarly, when I talk about business, I include all organisations. I know from working within the government and the public sector that they do consider themselves businesses too. Great HR is vital to all organisations.

Whatever your role or level, I urge you to challenge your ambition and your determination to make this relationship between HR and the business reap the richest harvest of its potential. You can't achieve the change you want by staying in your comfort zone, and I hope you will occasionally find your thoughts provoked. I will share my experiences and learning from my own HR roles and consultancy, with some questions for your own reflection. One size doesn't fit all.

I will help you to envision how you want HR to be regarded and woven into your organisation. I will offer practical approaches that you can explore in more depth via links to online resources if you wish. You will be able to build a framework for change, from strategic intent through to your important conversations.

I want this book to support you as a leader, as a professional and as a person. The human in all this is about more than resources. We're all in this together – making work work for the benefit of people and organisations.

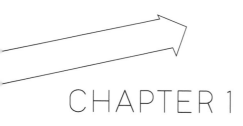

CHAPTER 1

A new era of work

A perfect storm is brewing in the world of work. Pressure is building from every direction – technological, social, demographic, economic and political. In today's global community of sharing and experimenting, fresh ideas and attitudes spread with amazing speed. Add to that the impetus created in 2020 by the global pandemic of coronavirus disease 2019 (Covid-19), and the result is an unstoppable momentum.

What does this mean for the HR function? This is a complex question that will enable us to open new and rigorous debates about human performance at work. Who owns it? Who enables it? Who motivates and inspires it? How can we measure it meaningfully? How can we create the best conditions for it?

Before we tackle these questions, let's take a deeper look at our changing world.

From loom to Zoom

It took a pandemic for us to realise that our mindset about work dates from a time when machinery was fixed, and bosses believed that workers couldn't be trusted. The first Industrial Revolution created cruel factories and workers who had to fight for respect. Looking at it that way, it's surprising that we hadn't already moved further from Arkwright's 1765 textile mill. Before then, people spun and wove at home.

Change has been slow, and this legacy has been holding us back in a comfort zone that is no longer comfortable for us or for the planet. We tend to value a familiar workplace where we can put our paper, pens and photos, but the people we need to work with are likely to be in a different location. Yet travelling to fixed locations for the traditional workday means commuting, sitting in traffic with thousands of others, day after day, making a journey that is potentially pointless.

We have made the leap into virtual working, and this has been an eye-opener. The technology works and we're learning that, in most cases, what we lose by not being in the same room is totally outweighed by the time and miles we save. Not just in the commuter journeys, but also in physical relocations of key people who, we believed, needed to move their entire families so that they could be in the office.

In my European HR role some years ago, I relocated many executives from one country to another. In organisations that claim to be global, it's strange that we've tended to think of relocating a whole family as demonstrating commitment to the role. I recall one case in particular where a sales director's relocation caused severe stress to his wife and five children and then, unsurprisingly, he wasn't successful in the role and was fired. It's typical of the HR role that you get to see the whole story, while the executive shows only their brave face to their boss.

Research into generational changes shows that younger people want to exercise much more choice and control and won't be pushed around. This also applies to when they choose to work. For them, the line between work and leisure is blurred: they expect to keep in touch with their lives on social media during the day, and they don't mind dipping into work outside official hours.

So, how do we measure productivity in a world in which we don't know and can't control when and where people are working? We know that what gets measured gets done, and even imperfect measures can provide real insight. What is it that we really value? This raises many questions about how we reward people, and for what.

Virtual working has proved that our ability to trust, and be trusted, has been underestimated. We're learning what we do need to control, and what we don't. Control and trust are an interesting double-act, and we'll come back to that later in this chapter. Measuring performance doesn't often need physical supervision, unless the role involves physical interaction; for example, a call-centre operator's performance can be tracked virtually during a call, while staff in hospitality or retail do benefit from observation when they're with the customer. For work in other sectors, such as construction, production or utilities, choices can be far more limited.

Global organisations tend to be ahead in this, using virtual working to service customers 24/7 with specialist teams who can 'follow the sun', that is, respond to calls from any time zone.

We've learned that working virtually can be made to work, and now can be a matter of choice rather than perceived operational need. A question for all of us to reflect on is where it does add value to be in close proximity, and where it doesn't.

As people at work, we've evolved

Let's look back for a moment at the archetype of workers in uniforms – whether bowler hats, flat caps or aprons – and compare that with the jeans and T-shirts that are acceptable today in most situations, even (if not especially) at corporate comms events. Our external appearances reveal radically changed attitudes towards class, status, compliance and deference. Allowing choice shows respect, and we have learned that self-esteem is core to performance.

The business rationale for diversity and inclusion (D&I) proves the commercial benefits of mirroring your organisation's market or community. The spirit of D&I teaches us how wonderful it is to embrace the talents, perspectives and values of all people. We're learning how powerful our unconscious bias is and, while there's still a long way to go, there is now a stronger groundswell than ever before for genuine equality.

Our young people have helped tremendously with this shift in attitude, and it runs alongside their stronger sense of individuality and self. Social media have been positive in creating stronger mutual support for this generation of people who have the means to find their 'tribe' anywhere in the world.

An interesting twist in this has been a change in how we expect trust to start; older generations believe it has to be earned, while research shows that younger people assume someone can be trusted unless they learn otherwise. It isn't just about age; attitudes now seem to be much more pliable across the board, probably because we're constantly consuming so much news and information direct from so many sources rather than having it mediated by others.

Connectivity to social media 24/7 brings us news, opinions and nonsense in a stream that's difficult to switch off. Our brains are constantly bombarded with stimulation, to a level that becomes unhealthy.

The amount of choice has exploded, across all aspects of life. Choice is now seen as a right, and it's difficult to take it away. Talented young people will not wait until someone else decides that they've earned the right for promotion – evidence shows that they feel less loyalty to their employer and more to their own career and their mastery of their work. While researching engagement at a video game company, we learned that coders were passionate about their work, not their company. As one Tomb Raider coder said to us, "I love Lara." Talented people in that sector tend to jump easily on to a new, exciting project with hardly a look back.

What does all this mean for the relationship we have with ourselves? Our struggle with mental health may not actually be any worse than it ever was, but it's certainly better understood. In so many ways, we're much more self-aware and conscious of the choices we make in life and in work – and more likely to feel frustration if we don't get them.

Employers' responsibilities towards mental wellbeing are now as stringent as they are towards physical health – and yet we need this relationship to be adult-adult rather than parental. A nurturing mindset can so easily undermine the spirit of individual accountability.

The complexity of all these changes in expectation, self-identity and trust varies from one organisation to another, and even within organisations. We recently ran the same management programme with a financial services organisation, where the senior managers in London were suited and sitting upright, while call centre managers elsewhere were dressed and seated casually. We can understand how the context and requirement for each of these roles varies, and how these play out in 'uniforms' and behaviour.

There is a new clarity and openness developing, with employers taking a fresh view of the whole person they need to fulfil the real requirements of a role. Decisions about recruitment and promotions are less tarnished by the paradigms of the past. In fact, the concept of the role itself may be challenged as a paradigm, as we now add technology into the mix.

Reimagining how work works

There is a strange disconnection here between what people say about technology transforming the way we work and what is actually happening. We read many more articles from suppliers about what's on offer than case studies of what's been done. I investigated this, and understood that, to truly benefit, organisations will have to totally rethink work and roles. It may not be possible to do it iteratively.

There are different levels of 'employing' technology; let's explore them.

Machine learning is well under way. We all know that the character who appears when we're on a website page isn't a real person, despite their name and cheery smile. These chatbots have learned from a real person (I'm oversimplifying here) until they could take on certain aspects of the interaction with a customer. The chatbot continues to learn and takes on more and more.

The next stage in machine learning is the progression to what tends to be called a bot. More of a personal assistant to a person, the bot learns from this person as it recognises repeated patterns of behaviour. This technology can facilitate knowledge management more comprehensively and protect an organisation from losing critical skills from expert workers. I'm guessing that you, like me, haven't heard of many actual examples of this.

Both of these examples are working 'around the edge' of the person's role, at the frontier of the interaction between the human brain and technology – I'm avoiding the term 'artificial intelligence' (AI) because the experts would say that it is used wrongly in this context. They're based on our existing paradigm that the human is at the centre of the work and that the technology can be deployed to help them.

If we want to truly embrace this opportunity, we have to throw up into the air all our preconceived ideas about roles and, instead, focus on the work – the tasks, the component parts, the processes and the problem we're actually trying to solve. Only then can we decide how best to apply human intelligence and computer intelligence, respectively.

Here's the challenge for HR. Consider your HR function. To what extent is it:

    a. redesigning its own processes, services and interactions?

    b. enabling the organisation to redesign work?

Tackling a) has achieved great progress, for example, with the development of employee apps that act as portals for them to draw in helpful services and self-manage data, to access FAQs and tips for managing people, and to navigate internal resources.

It's harder to achieve b). The suppliers are ready and impatient, painting exciting pictures of what they could do, but the actual case studies are, again, hard to find.

Recreating processes strategically is one thing, and we have the systems architecture and mindset for that. Tearing up a whole-organisation system of roles and accountabilities is much harder. The core questions would be:

- What is the problem that we want to solve here?
- How can we best apply computer intelligence to this problem?
- How can we best apply human intelligence?

When we think of how organisations are currently organised, the problem – how we develop products, produce them or respond to customers – is actually spread among many roles, hence the difficulty in even getting started. In fact, the way we see the problem may itself need to be torn apart.

Therefore, making the best use of the amazing technologies being developed cannot be done piecemeal. In our heads, are we still in Arkwright's factory, with the same mental concept of responsibilities and rewards, and the need for some kind of comfort zone that's based on our specialist expertise? How would we feel if the concept of having a role were taken away?

This is exciting and a little scary. What kind of transformation of attitudes will be required to strip apart everything that we're used to? What kind of leadership will that demand? The human contribution will always be the most individual and indispensable, but will itself need to be re-engineered, recrafted and realigned.

The role of HR to lead this is clearly pivotal but must be grasped before it is taken away. There is much technical genius being applied to the redesign of work, and new roles envisioned to manage the integration, translation and taxonomy of new technologies.

The only way to ensure that these developments are strategic and cohesive is to take an organisation-wide approach. Only HR has the oversight, reach and expertise to work with leaders to join up all elements. Don't let the busy-ness of existing HR responsibilities undermine your organisation's abilities to grasp these exciting technological advances.

Fundamental changes to power and control

Cultural change is already well under way. Social media have made so many things so much more transparent. We can see through people, organisations, claims and constructs. We're much more likely to ask, "What's the real point of this?" and to be able to see that the emperor is not wearing any clothes. Advertisers know that today's audiences are cynical, and in the same way employees are now much more educated consumers of employment, careers and leadership.

We can check out the private, actual actions of an organisation and its leaders almost as easily as those they choose to put into the public domain. Organisations know now that stating or redefining their values must be more than a public image exercise, and that these values must be lived. This is complex and much more difficult than putting a poster on the wall. It's a subtle mix of behaviours, routines, rhythms and symbols.

For example, when working with a pensions company I wanted to research the actual values they had in place before facilitating the process of crafting a set of values they would publish and 'live'. We put together a team of 'culture vultures' whose job was to observe and pick out examples of what was valued and drawn to attention in normal, day-to-day life. The exercise was instructive.

One telling example was that teams would have a special lunch when someone left. Nothing unusual in that, except that they didn't do the same when someone joined. Digging deeper revealed that the leaving parties were organised by colleagues, rather than managers. Looking further into this, we discovered that not only were joiners not socialised into their teams, but most managers didn't organise social get-togethers at all. Natural rhythms like that tell us much about what is valued – or not.

Turning values into policies is a core activity for HR that is valuable for transparency. In many organisations, however, these look dated. The truth is that most policies are written by the previous generation to those most affected by them, and generational difference has never been more marked than it is now.

Policies do give organisations power, much of which comes from law and governance as well as commercial need and probity. They also present an important opportunity to get guidelines across in a way that reflects the culture and values you want in your organisation.

People can see through words and actions, and leaders' integrity and authenticity are tested as never before. We accept less at face value and are alert to the signs of cultivated behaviours, such as, "My boss actually listened to me this morning; they must have been on a training course." This has, I am sure, always been the case, but only recently has the risk been so great of reputational damage via social media. One clever meme or video can go viral overnight.

We are measured by our actions, not by our intentions.

Today, building a culture of autonomy and individual accountability is wise in many organisations, especially those that employ knowledge workers. However, organisations were based on the family structure: it's our natural environment, and these dynamics are incredibly powerful. In any situation it is easy to fall into behavioural patterns that draw from parents and children, and this doesn't stop when we're at work. This is more subtle in organisations, but it means either assuming responsibility for others, as parents do, or allowing others to take it from us, as children do.

Berne's well-known theory of transactional analysis (see Resources) is a cornerstone of the work that I and many others do with leaders one-to-one and in workshops to help them to understand this dynamic. Put simply, if someone speaks to us with the tone that a parent would use, we're hardwired to be triggered as a child, and vice versa. Once caught in that spiral, we become as frustrated with ourselves as with the other party. Learning to control that can help us enormously to get the outcome we wanted from the conversation.

Understanding this is vital to understanding how power and control play out at work. Feeling that you have an adult-to-adult relationship with your boss is something that talented and self-respecting people value, and it creates the foundation for them to give their best. This adult-adult relationship is something that can be part of organisational cultures too – being treated as an adult is the way things are done around here. Power is shared, as is autonomy, and that means that accountability is shared too.

Let's not pretend that this is easy, however, especially for HR – from their strategy through to how they interact with line managers.

On the one hand, we want employees to feel responsible for their own performance and careers – that's good for everyone. On the other hand, as employers, we're obliged legally, ethically and morally to feel responsible for our employees' wellbeing as well as performance. There are occasions when we need to point out what's right or wrong, steer behaviour and correct it. The fact that this often falls to HR to do is part of their challenge and we will look further at this in Chapter 7, which deals with **Balance**.

How are you using your power as employers? This may be a rather difficult question for you to answer but look for signs of this in how you operate as an organisation, as well as in the relationship between power and responsibility. Balancing power and responsibility is challenging. You may have the power to do something, but should you? What are the full implications of using your power in this way? There may be a dilemma between the benefit in the short term, getting this issue sorted right now, and the longer term, building the lasting culture that will support your sustained success as an organisation.

We'll come back to this dilemma, but the reason for raising it here is that people of all ages, but especially the young, demand to be treated as adults. Employees are more questioning and challenging, and less accepting of seniority. Organisations have to work harder and more consciously at living the 'right' or appropriate values because they will be called out if they don't.

These changes in technology, working practices, attitudes and power combine to demand a fundamental rewiring in organisations. They present a once-in-a-career opportunity for HR and business leaders to collaborate in new ways, and to redefine the way they work together.

Most importantly, they must take the opportunity to lead together: to demonstrate that creating the conditions for high performance, enjoyment and success at work is a responsibility shared by all.

Whether you are a business or HR leader, here are some questions for you to consider:

- How quickly is your organisation responding to technological opportunities?

- What have you learned, for yourself, about where proximity is vital, versus working virtually?

- Thinking of recent meetings, what generational differences have you observed?

- What tone do you use in your messaging a) as an organisation; and b) personally, as a leader? When are the occasions when you are most likely to slip into 'parent'?

- What matters most to you as a person? To what extent is the answer different when you consider being a) at home; and b) at work?

CHAPTER 2

Leading the people agenda

Whose responsibility is it to ensure that people perform at their best in organisations? This is a central question in this book, and it's complex. For example, in a recent article an author stated, "HR has failed to reduce harassment in organisations," and this is typical of the lack of understanding that exists about how HR actually works. In the background, in many private conversations that can't be advertised, HR people will have been doing their best to influence and coach those doing the harassment to change their behaviour. However, if it's systemic then we must look at the whole system.

Aside from administration, the HR function achieves nothing alone. It creates best practice, and is a channel through which this is developed and disseminated through leaders and managers across the organisation. However sound their expertise and advice, if the HR people's relationship with business leaders is not built on respect and credibility, they will be unable to influence. HR is in a kind of supply chain, where its impact on business results is achieved through actions that others take – or don't take, if we use the harassment example.

The only way for organisations to achieve high performance in people is through true partnership and shared accountability between HR and business leaders, with alignment at all levels. This is largely accepted, in theory. In practice, we've been trying for decades to make it happen. The people agenda must be led from the top, accepting the concept that it is the partnership between HR and line managers that turns intent into reality.

This is the point at which we drive the return on investment for HR. This is where HR's credibility lives.

Embrace business realities

"I'm a business leader who happens to be in HR," is a sound attitude from HR directors. HR needs to be pragmatic, realistic, and front and centre of delivery to customers. Business results are the ultimate measure of HR's success too. This must be HR's starting point.

What drives success, and how can we get more of it? Every organisation has its own distinctive business model – its own formula of ingredients and how they're mixed. For example, a high-margin business will have a completely different tolerance to expenses from one that is low-margin. There is no right answer to how measures are identified and used, but I've seen some rather simplistic examples that do little to explain to employees how a business works and, therefore, what's important.

I worked with a logistics company for several years, where the finance director's favourite measure of performance was the cost per mile to run their vehicles. I'm not a financial expert – but I wanted them to talk more about customers than about lorries.

Measures give powerful messages about what's important and are important tools for communication. The business reality for them, however, was that they had very tight margins and little room to manoeuvre.

HR people must demonstrate that they understand the tough stuff and create explicit links between investment in people interventions and the hard outcomes. In my conversation with the logistics company finance director, I had to speak his language, not mine. "Cost per mile is important, and the way the driver interacts with the customer is vital to that. You know that you lose customers because of poor service. Your costs per mile are based on full lorries. When you lose a customer, the cost recovery of those trips is lost because they're going half empty. Your cost per mile effectively doubles."

We worked with the board to research engagement. The results showed that the drivers felt frustrated and undervalued. At the same time, they had administrative issues with proof of delivery, which meant not being paid. We looked into it and, as is so often the case, found that the drivers themselves were full of ideas and real commitment to make things work better. The most vocal complainers can often prove to be those who care the most and have the most to offer. They'd been ignored. We ran some process improvement sessions, with sticky notes covering large sheets of brown paper, and generated practical ideas that the drivers bought into and stuck to. Engagement went up, driver retention went up, and customer satisfaction went up too.

As a result, the company put together a balanced scorecard that encompassed the enablers as well as the outcomes, for example, the quality of line management as well as profit. A challenge for HR is that most of its work is around the enablers and can be hard to quantify. We will come back to this as well as the topic of business acumen in Chapter 6, which looks at **Perspective**.

HR language is valid, for example, retention, turnover, and especially the cost of recruiting new drivers. When you're making the case for a business investment, however, you have to make a business case. You learn the language from being in the meetings, listening to the arguments, picking up the stress points. Speaking the right language gets you into the meetings too. It demonstrates that you do, truly, understand business realities. It's a virtuous circle and leads to HR being seen as a true partner in business success.

How strategic is your HR function?

The reach of the HR function extends into the work and lives of every employee, and yet the vast majority of those people do not report to HR. HR is required to influence actions, attitudes and behaviours – the soft stuff that wise people realise is actually the hard stuff. HR creates a framework, or fabric, to build the culture that the business needs, and it needs everyone to line up behind that, at every level. The fabric will contain various threads of interventions, projects and guidelines that need to be woven together by line managers.

This is why the relationship between the chief executive and the chief HR officer or HR director is critical. How well do they understand each other – their respective priorities, concerns and ways of seeing the organisation? How deep is the chief executive's insight into what truly enables human performance, and how savvy is the HR director about what drives the optimum business result? The quality of this dialogue about human and business outcomes is vital.

The chief executive needs to hear the truth, and this job often falls to the HR director. Board colleagues have their own agenda, and the chief executive needs a trusted partner, sounding board and honest arbiter. In return, the HR director wins their own hearing.

The truth is, not every chief executive 'gets' HR in all its depth and breadth, and not every HR director is good at using the right language and data to illustrate the connections between people and business outcomes. We will return to this later, particularly in Chapter 10, which is about **Focus**.

The challenge is to ensure that HR strategy is totally aligned with, and actively supported by, the business. There is much excellent expertise that HR specialists offer – recruiting, developing and retaining the talent you need – and it can take on a language of its own that creates a subtle barrier. The 'ivory tower' of HR is something that everyone wants to avoid, yet it can happen easily by default when anyone takes on the role of expert or adviser, or fails to involve key stakeholders early enough in designing a new intervention.

Building a cohesive strategy depends on pulling together many perspectives. Conflict and ambiguity are everywhere in organisations and it can be difficult to navigate a clear way forward. The most effective use of a leader's time is to create clarity – once people are clear about where they are headed, they can work productively. Both business and HR strategies should be jointly led, so that you explain together what the business needs to deliver, and what you expect from people to achieve that. Without this top-level partnership it is impossible for HR strategy to *be* fully strategic.

A powerful way to achieve this clear and visible alignment is to use the technique of storytelling to create a strategic narrative – first for the business, and then for HR, which will fit together like two spoons.

Let's use examples to illustrate how this can work. Here I am imagining a high-tech company. In your own organisation, you would make this far more relevant. Crafting it together, in a collaboration between HR and business, can be a powerful activity that builds shared ownership.

> Organisation:
> "Our technology improves lives around the world."
>
> Strategic HR:
> "We create the conditions for expertise to thrive."
>
> HR business partners:
> "We build bridges towards great people outcomes."

This can be cascaded through the levels and divisions of an organisation, to create absolute clarity about where HR adds value within that overarching narrative. You can bring people together to do this in a powerful workshop – to talk about what this means in practice for their team. Then you can invite individuals to consider their personal leadership narrative within this context, for example, "I build and share my own talents."

This ownership of the people agenda is most powerful when it is strategic, operational and personal. Then it can be lived in every interaction. People across the organisation start to sit up and notice a change, and with persistence this shift can become transformational and thus truly strategic. We will come back to transformational HR in Chapter 8, which talks about **Push**.

Building productive partnerships at every level

Getting the most from your people is a multi-level partnership that must be led from the top. Let's take the example of treating people inclusively. Strategy, values, policies – they start out as aspirations, get turned into documents, and achieve absolutely nothing until they are made real at the front line. They rely on the actions of managers, day in, day out. As mentioned earlier, HR has no authority over managers; theirs is a challenge of influence and education.

Business partnering is an inspired concept created by thought leader and author Dave Ulrich (see Resources). He recognised the complexity of all the varied HR responsibilities and clarified a structure that would separate three areas: the administrative processes, often called shared services; the generalist support to the line manager, often called the HR business partner; and the centres of expertise, where specialists in areas such as recruitment, reward, organisation design and talent management reside.

Dave Ulrich was, however, the first to point out that the transition to the role of HR business partner is far more difficult than changing the job title. The first session of our workshops on this role always has to be 'What *is* business partnering?' The truth is that organisations decide how they want this to work, and even HR business partners within the same organisation often work differently from one another.

Business partnering is a role, not a job title. It's an attitude and an ambition as well as a set of skills and behaviours. It supports any generalist or specialist role, in HR or other central or professional functions such as finance or information technology (IT).

In this chapter, I will explore how it fits within the leading the people agenda, and in the chapters about our seven HR Enablers will look in more detail at how to make it work in practice.

The essence of partnering is that it demands an equal relationship – a sharing of what each partner is best at. The 'line' leader or manager brings their deep understanding of how their part of the organisation works, and of the individuals in their team. The HR manager (who may or may not have the HR business partner job title, but let's use it for simplicity) brings their professional expertise and, often, a broad insight into different client groups, with a close connection to organisational values and how to live these. What they should both become clear about, together, is what drives success. What are the business outcomes that must be delivered, and what is it that people need to do, or be, to achieve those?

Where you have the strategic clarity of message on both sides that I mentioned earlier, there is a stronger platform for robust dialogue about how to drive the business and the people outcomes. Are these outcomes different? Unfortunately, yes; this is just one of the inherent tensions. For example, driving productivity could be at the expense of employee engagement. It's a constant balancing act.

Let's take a call centre I spoke to yesterday about my insurance. I could tell that the very helpful and professional adviser, Sue, was torn between managing the call quickly and being friendly. She sounded like the kind of person who was far more motivated by building a relationship with me as a customer than getting me off the call – but she had to do the latter to meet her targets. I'd guess she's already looking for a role where she can be more of her true self. For her line manager, she may even be a performance issue if she's failing to meet her targets.

Let's imagine that Sue's line manager (we'll call him Pete) decides to talk to his HR business partner about her. This is a classic example of a tactical HR issue, where the HR person may advise Pete about his options, and steps to take to turn the situation around with

Sue or, if things are at a late stage, follow disciplinary procedures correctly. If this is as far as the conversation goes, it isn't partnering. It is valid, and valuable, but it is transactional.

Let's look briefly at the difference between transactional and transformational. When an interaction is transactional, it can be effective but nothing significant changes as a result. Pete will resolve the issue with Sue, by following the HR business partner's advice. The HR business partner achieves something more *transformational* when they challenge Pete's thinking, use their coaching skills to help Pete develop, and take a broader and deeper look at what's happening. In fact, it turns out that Pete's real issue is his relationship with his boss, who is dictating performance targets that Pete himself feels are unfair.

Our HR business partner enables Pete to prepare for a conversation with his boss so that he can tackle his frustration with his own performance targets. HR is clear, in values terms, that its leadership would want Pete to feel he could tackle this. Pete had been feeling like a victim, and uncomfortable with the way he'd felt obliged to treat Sue. For the moment, let's trust that Pete's boss handles this well, and that they find a way forward that works for them both. This has the potential to be transformational: their relationship, and Pete's skills and confidence, have moved forward.

There is a difficult time dynamic in moving from transactional to transformational; it takes longer for the HR business partner to coach Pete, but the outcome is that he is more self-sufficient in future.

I mentioned earlier the dilemma of choosing between the short term and the long term, and there is a strong link between this and the parent-child dynamic. They build into an effective mix of intellectual and behavioural choices which we will continue to explore in this book. Intellectually, we know that when we help the other person to think they will own their decisions and actions. Behaviourally, this takes some self-control – 'telling' can seem easier and quicker when you're busy.

A closer two-way partnership also avoids the time-wasting that arises when HR finds out late about a forthcoming change and finds itself in catch-up mode.

Our HR business partner achieved leadership in their conversation with Pete. They enabled him and supported him, while leaving the responsibility for the outcome with him. They avoided the tendency to look only at the immediate problem, and they widened the horizon. There is often a conflict between a short-term quick fix, and a more lasting solution. HR has strong credibility in Pete's organisation and so he listened to Sue: that is another factor we will explore later.

Imagine what can be delivered by having these high-quality relationships in place at every level, between HR and business leaders and managers: professionals who seek genuinely to understand each other's worlds, to apply their own expertise and insight generously, and to generate ideas and innovations that add real value and growth to people and the business.

When the chief executive and HR director work together to support this kind of productive partnership, they enable transformation to happen. It is through these relationships, supported by strategic alignment, that HR earns the right and ability to lead.

What drives human performance outcomes?

It's a snappy question that disguises deep complexity. HR people study this and tend to understand it instinctively but have to make it explicit and explain the connections. Only then can they hold line leaders and managers accountable for their part of it.

This clarity has to start with understanding the financial picture. HR must speak the right language – EBITDA (earnings before interest, taxes, depreciation and amortisation), CSFs (critical success factors), KPIs (key performance indicators), NPS (Net Promoter Score®) and so forth – and be able to relate their arguments, issues and concerns to those.

Here's a powerful way to illustrate the connections between enablers and outcomes. It builds on work done by the European Foundation for Quality Management (EFQM) and Tomorrow's Company:

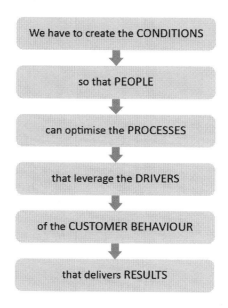

You can see the flow of the activities that ultimately drive the business results you need. When creating strategy, however, you start from the bottom and work upwards. For example:

- What are the absolute results we must deliver? (eg shareholder value, profit, brand)

- What is the customer behaviour that creates those results? (eg buy, buy more, tell others)

- What are the drivers of that customer behaviour? (eg product design, availability, customer service)

- What are the processes that leverage these drivers of customer behaviour? (eg electronic point of sale, website, merchandising)

- What enables people to leverage these processes and/or get more of the desired customer behaviour? (eg training, role clarity, effective line management)

- What are the conditions that need to be in place for those things to happen? (eg culture, leadership, values)

You can see that this is a useful way to make the connections. Going back to our logistics company, leaders learned that by improving the conditions of trust and involvement within their culture they improved processes, which enabled them to give better customer service as well as improve margins. The root cause of the issue was, they realised, the underlying condition of a lack of respect for the importance of drivers. Their HR manager had known that, of course, but had to make a business case for it. Having achieved this, he could also win support and budget for training the drivers' managers.

Securing a budget for developing people tends to be a real test of an organisation's understanding of the value of people. Early on in my career as a consultant, a technical director asked me why he should train people in anything other than their technical skills. I was totally unprepared for the question, because it was obvious to me. I wish I'd used an analogy that he would have understood – that of investing in IT.

IT is on a capital budget that isn't often challenged, while headcount costs are. Upgrades for your IT system are also unlikely to be challenged – everyone accepts that IT is critical to competitive advantage. If someone damages a computer, they're likely to get into a lot of trouble. When someone leaves, their manager isn't likely to be reprimanded.

People cost more than IT, and yet we can be careless with this precious resource. Interestingly, huge advancements in artificial intelligence (AI) will make the human factor even more important, not less.

Leading the people agenda demands a firm grasp of the numbers and the interplay between hard and soft, outcomes and enablers. Debating, negotiating and agreeing on an ethical, practical and meaningful set of measures at the top level creates a clear framework not only for measuring productivity, but also for communicating what's important. When HR people incorporate financial vocabulary in their daily language, they demonstrate their connection to business realities and create common ground.

Many HR leaders will be fully cognisant of the financial fundamentals, but not start there. This can change. Start by talking about business first, and HR second. The realities of every business are, in fact, fascinating, and create their own case for good HR.

The transformational HR leader

People have high expectations of HR leaders. As well as applying their functional expertise, they are the arbiters of all that is good and fair in the organisation. They are senior coaches, sounding boards and referees. They must be role models for the organisation's values, and be squeaky clean – after all, at times they are required to make some delicate judgments about what's right and wrong. They also have the reputation of the HR function in their hands and a powerful impact on those partnerships between HR and the business at every level. They need to be a clear, strong voice on the board, invited to every important discussion.

These are heavy responsibilities, and it requires a strong sense of self to carry them – a sense of comfort and confidence in who you are as a leader. This means finding your own way of *being* in the role, and in your relationship with the chief executive. Authenticity and trust are popular leadership concepts yet take hard work to earn.

It is true of all leadership roles that the complexity increases as you progress up the ladder, and this is why you need a strong centre of gravity. Leaders also need to challenge the practices and routines they have developed – their default. I am privileged to run a challenging, self-awareness leadership programme with a global organisation. In that, we explore together, in a supportive environment, a leader's personal leadership journey. First, we illuminate the kind of leader they are actually being and review how they feel about that and to what extent this is working for them. Second, we explore the leader they want to be and how to achieve that.

Reviewing our *practices* is valuable – this is what we do first on that programme. It means taking an honest look at what we actually do – not what we know we should do or want to do – but our *actual* practices. The leaders analyse what this means in terms of the percentage of time they are actually leading, versus managing – and they invariably decide they want to do more leading.

The extra challenge in this for HR leaders is in the nature of the services they provide for their organisation. In HR, you do not know what kind of issue is going to arise on any given day – performance problems, grievances, bereavements, physical or emotional illness, legal matters – alongside various projects and interventions that you may be rolling out. When someone appears at your door, you don't always have the option of scheduling a meeting in three days' time, because you can tell that this person needs to talk to you right now, or you are concerned that a situation may blow up.

Operational HR issues can create a gravitational pull into a reactive spiral. The challenge for HR to be proactive is a long-standing struggle. Sadly, you don't build leadership credibility by being known as a problem-solver: you make it harder to establish.

Transformational HR takes strong leadership, and courage at every level. The value of great HR and its strategic purpose must be recognised and advocated by leaders in every function. Driving high-performance outcomes is a partnership in which every stakeholder must play their full part.

Seismic shifts are taking place in the world of work. HR as a function must lead in designing the future vision of work by role modelling the partnerships and collaboration that will create the right vision and then turn it into reality. HR leaders are business leaders first.

Whether you are a leader of business or HR, here are some questions for you to consider:

- What does HR business partnering mean in your organisation?

- What are the business imperatives that people talk about most in your organisation?

- What contribution do you make towards these in your role?

- What are the central messages that you want people to receive about HR and the people agenda?

- How would people describe you as a leader?

CHAPTER 3

What the business needs from HR

A lot of people have opinions about HR: "HR should… ," or, "HR must…". Many are highly qualified to comment, as they represent business leaders. Some opinions reveal a lack of understanding of how HR works in practice. What we have learned from HR people themselves, in fact, is that they want to change too. Therefore, there is a happy alignment in that both business leaders and HR see a need for change. There is less clarity about how to achieve that. That is what we have researched and continue to explore.

Effective HR has never been so important, as you will have seen in Chapter 1. Demographic, generational, technological and social changes are combining in ways that put human performance even more at the forefront. HR must be at the centre of working this out at the strategic level, understanding what it will take to ensure that we are getting best value from human intelligence.

The research behind our seven HR Enablers

We kept hearing HR people say, "We know we need to change, but we don't know how." Our mission was to reveal the things that were under the control of HR people, that they could work on, personally and as a team, whatever their level.

There are so many dimensions within HR and, as explored in Chapter 2, it is vital to illuminate what really matters. What makes HR work better? How could we help HR people to shift how they operate? It's a very busy job – we can't magic up more time. What we could do, however, was to work out what they could do more of, and less of, to be more successful and feel more valued.

There are many specialisms – employee relations, talent, reward, organisational development, learning and development, and more – and HR has deep understanding of these. This technical expertise isn't the issue. HR is rarely criticised for developing solutions that aren't best practice. When it is criticised, it is more likely to be for seeming to be out of step with the business, not speaking the right language or putting obstacles in the way.

The impact of this is that interventions are not readily embraced; employment law advice is resisted; HR is caught on the back foot because it wasn't involved early enough; line managers pay lip service to HR policies and don't own them. In summary, line managers can feel that HR is not on their side.

The underlying issue behind all these concerns is the quality of the interaction between HR and the business. One way to look at HR is as a kind of gateway – a channel through which good things can pass into the business, to enrich it and drive results. If the gate is closed, or even only part way open, then HR cannot fully do its job.

So, if we could enable HR people to improve this relationship, it would improve everything else.

We pooled our experiences and trawled through a myriad of white papers, reports, articles and comments from business leaders and opinion leaders. Many prestigious organisations – including Deloitte, PwC, Korn Ferry and KPMG – regularly share their thinking on what HR should be doing, and, most importantly, Dave Ulrich at The RBL Group homes in on HR's capabilities (see Resources). Ulrich saw the structural response I mentioned earlier, with HR business partners being only part of the solution, and he continues to encourage and contribute to the debate. Professional institutes are also a key source of insight; in particular, the UK's Chartered Institute of Personnel and Development (CIPD) offers a comprehensive profession map: https://www.cipd.co.uk/professionmap

These are all valuable inputs, but they don't all agree and many use strategic language that's difficult to translate into operational reality and observable competencies. We wanted to work out where to get real traction, which is why we made our focus clear and practical:

> What is it that makes the interaction between HR and the business effective, so that the best outcomes can be achieved? What does it look like? How can we measure it?

We wanted to develop something that HR people could use, in the most practical sense, to shift how they operate. From all the research, we distilled the activities and behaviours that combine to build the relationship between HR and the business. They fell into seven themes, or 'enablers', which we will explore individually in the next seven chapters.

Reputation
Winning respect as a valued contributor to business success is built on the quality of HR's relationships; raising their profile as a function as well as having positive impact with authentic personal leadership.

Connection
Making and nurturing the right connections across the business to help HR to target and deliver services in the most effective way possible; earning a seat at the table; political savvy.

Perspective
Taking a step back – systematically gathering and updating the information that enables HR to make robust decisions and engage others' support, developing insight and acting accordingly.

Balance
This is about steering a path that values the needs of all stakeholders; developing approaches that stick; taking the long-term view while role modelling the organisation's values.

Push
HR faces complex challenges – it's about more than the numbers, it's about hearts and minds, and behaviours. HR needs to push forwards, and at times also push back – to stand up and speak out.

Rigour
HR can't pass 'go' without the credibility that comes from reliable, accurate and up-to-date operational and advisory services - delivering what they promise day in, day out, getting it right and making it better.

Focus
Taking the insight that's been gathered, and using that to make sure that HR's efforts and resources are invested in the right areas - in order to get the best value for the business.

Experience of working with these seven HR Enablers has proved them to be robust. To explore more about how they are used in evaluation of self, team and 360, and in our workshops, please visit our website: https://www.enable-hr.com

The interaction between HR and the business

When we travel around the world, even now, we need to take our plug adapters. If our plug doesn't fit into the socket, electricity cannot flow into our vital equipment and gadgets. We never think to ourselves, "How stupid; the people in this country should change their sockets so that my plug will fit." If an HR intervention is not appropriate, the result is that the positive energy from it cannot flow – or possibly there will be a reduced supply or even a painful shock.

My first hard lesson in this was some years ago, when competency frameworks were a new HR tool. They offered real clarity for required performance levels, development plans and career paths. I spent many hours crafting seven levels of skill across something like 32 behaviours for salespeople. You can imagine how invested in it I was after all that work.

I took it to my European client groups. In Rome, Antonio said, "Yes, Debbie, we will use this." In Frankfurt, Erik said, "Debbie, we don't need this, and we aren't going to do it." In fact, Antonio didn't implement it either. Apart from the lesson in working with different cultures, it was a lesson in influencing – or failing to.

Let's think of questions that may help us here. How do we make our plug fit the socket? How do we alter the socket so that our plug will fit? Can we make it work if we use more force? Of course, none of these questions will produce a complete answer. We have to go back several steps.

The global analogy is a useful one, as something that works in one country, or company, may not be successfully adopted in another. Working cross-culturally is a wonderful lesson in understanding that there is no right or wrong about what works where. Cultures, companies, departments and teams have their own ways of working and have built up their own beliefs about what matters. Added to that, they're busy and they don't like change and hassle.

Here's a different way of looking at the challenge. What we need to work out is how to build the channel so that the energy can flow both ways. This human energy can be as powerful as electricity; made up of intellectual sharing and challenging, robust debate, generous curiosity and learning; teamwork and fun. When you build into this chemistry the deep insight that each side brings – of their market, product, customer, technology and professional specialism – you have a formula that can win in any sector.

Our seven enablers provide a framework for tackling this vital interaction between HR and the business. They explore the practical activities that underpin HR's credibility: the way the transactional services and advice are given, accurately and reliably, through to the elements that drive HR's reputation throughout the business and drive transformation. They can be applied at any level of role, and strategically as well as tactically. Most importantly, they are measurable: you can tell whether or not they are happening.

We looked at some activities that are crucial and broke them down into their key components. This makes it easier to evaluate whether they happen or not.

We analysed success as a kind of process, eg influencing:

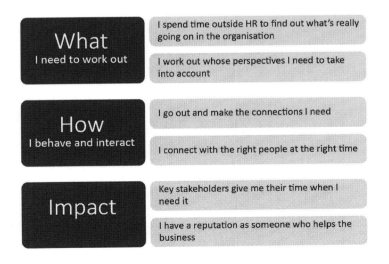

What
I need to work out

- I spend time outside HR to find out what's really going on in the organisation
- I work out whose perspectives I need to take into account

How
I behave and interact

- I go out and make the connections I need
- I connect with the right people at the right time

Impact

- Key stakeholders give me their time when I need it
- I have a reputation as someone who helps the business

As I mentioned earlier, there is no magic wand to create more time. Our aim is to enable you to make conscious choices about how you operate, so that you can make a shift. This is why we use the frequency scale in our evaluation tool:

This helps you decide whether you want more of this, or less. The additional questions below the slider further enable you to highlight what you choose to work on.

The question above is an example of what we call an 'output' question: it offers a test on how productive your relationships are. This also illustrates how useful it can be to ask stakeholders for their view on the same statements in a 360-degree version.

It can also be surprising how perceptions in the same team vary. Sharing perceptions and debating priorities provides an opportunity to realign them around what will add most value.

As we go through the following chapters on the seven HR Enablers, we will further explore the activities and behaviours that support productive relationships and offer some techniques.

This critical interaction can't be outsourced

So many aspects of HR can be outsourced. HR technology is growing rapidly, and administrative functions can be handed over to expert centres. Specialist projects can be given to external consultants who bring in depth of expertise as well as experience from other organisations. However, the vital relationship between HR and the business – that critical partnership that enables high performance from people, day in, day out, on the ground – cannot be outsourced.

Nor can you outsource making sure that the best return on investment (ROI) is achieved in people outcomes. That's key in tailoring interventions, whether it's on a large scale, such as the architecture of a career structure, or local training. These are HR-led – they bring new ideas and expertise into the organisation. However, they are plugs and may not be appropriate for the socket. They may be beautifully crafted, like my aforementioned competency framework, but not fit for purpose or well positioned to be adopted.

There are also many day-to-day interactions around operational and performance issues. HR needs to be on the ground, closely connected, in order to facilitate sound decisions and actions. These conversations and meetings are where these HR Enablers are lived.

HR learns constantly about its leaders and managers from these meetings and conversations. It learns about the health of culture and engagement, and organisational effectiveness. Its insights feed upwards to inform and qualify HR initiatives.

The business imperatives will always have a louder voice, and quite rightly so. They are driven by market realities and the need for financial growth and sustainability. The most valued HR people will be those who play the role of translator and facilitator, supporting leaders and managers as they navigate the complexities of getting the most from people in their particular context.

In the next seven chapters, I will explore our HR Enablers and how they build into this effective, productive and rewarding partnership.

CHAPTER 4

Reputation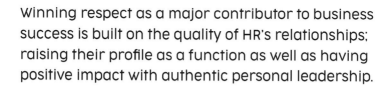

Winning respect as a major contributor to business success is built on the quality of HR's relationships; raising their profile as a function as well as having positive impact with authentic personal leadership.

What do you want your HR function to be known for?

There are so many interactions, every day, between HR and people at every level in the organisation. Some interactions are person-to-person, between the HR leader or professional and the employee, but most are one step removed – they're HR's advice or policies being put into practice by someone else. The tentacles of HR reach into every aspect of organisational life, and it's difficult to see how you can control how they play out – not only whether the right thing happens, in the right way, but whether it's *seen* to happen. This perception can impact on the whole organisation's reputation externally, as well as that of HR.

Reputation is absolutely core to HR's ability to deliver. The great test is what people say about you when you're *not* in the room. Is it likely to be, "HR does a great job"? Not a bad obituary – it would certainly open the door to meetings at the operational level. How much better to hear, "HR shows great leadership," or "HR proves how pivotal it is to our success," or even, "HR is front and centre, strategically as well as operationally." You can see how the last judgment would ensure the door to the top-level meetings always being open.

HR is being watched all the time, at every level

This is why HR needs to be fully conscious of the strategy and the tactics of building its credibility and influence. Reputation is hard-won and can be lost in a heartbeat. HR needs a risk strategy for how it is regarded, in the same way as an organisation does.

Let's look first at the strategic aspects of this. In Chapter 2 we looked at the strategic narrative for HR, and this is a good place to start. We'll work with our HR narrative from earlier and get creative with it. You would select the appropriate level, for example:

> Strategic HR:
> "We create the conditions for expertise to thrive," or

> HR business partners:
> "We build bridges towards great people outcomes."

What will this look like, when it is fully achieved? In an HR team alignment workshop, we used the exercise of envisioning this, on a flipchart, as an animal. They imagined:

- what it looks like (eg powerful, streamlined, elegant, cat-like, could pounce and turn quickly; had sleek fur but claws that it could show when it needed)

- its environment (sunny, warm, some tropical gardens and a nice beach, with some shady places to rest)

- what it eats (data, evidence, success stories, reality)

- how it feels about itself (proud, confident, but humble)

- how others behave when it is around (welcoming, involving, respectful).

This visual image was captured digitally and used over a long period to remind the HR team of their vision, and to measure how they were doing in their journey towards it. It continued to inspire them, and keep them on the same page, as they turned it into reality.

We don't start with a blank page when we are working out how to build our reputation. There are many preconceptions already out there, and they're probably not consistent. When you ask someone, "What do you think of HR?" they are likely to evaluate the HR person that they have the most contact with. We've heard people say, "I don't rate HR, but I do value my HR business partner," and also the other way around. Some people in the HR business partner role can 'go native'; that is, build a stronger relationship with their client group than they have with their central HR function. This is another difficult path to tread: it requires skill and a strong strategic message (such as our HR narrative) for HR professionals to keep in mind to ensure they can be loyal to both.

Beliefs drive reputation

This works on at least three different levels: organisational, functional and personal. First, let's look at the beliefs that exist in the organisation about the HR function. This is an important question when we are considering HR's reputation. Beliefs drive behaviour, and behaviour drives reputation. If the chief executive has positive beliefs about HR, this will show in their behaviour and attitude towards HR people and what they do.

Second, what about the beliefs HR leaders have about their own function? Our beliefs leak. If HR leaders themselves believe fully that HR has real value and is vital to success, that will come across in everything that they do.

This leads us to the third and most vital area: the beliefs you have about yourself. If you don't believe it, you can't *be* it. A myriad of individual signals, such as tone of voice, movement and body language, build into a picture of your overall *being* that is received and quickly but subconsciously interpreted into an impression that sticks. Let's look further at this personal aspect of reputation.

The impression people have of you gets passed around, and it's a shortcut that we need to influence. People may say, "Oh yes, Greta, you can always rely on her," or, "Mike, he's really going places," or, "Hans, he's competent but so quiet." In leadership programmes, once a supportive climate has been fully created so that people will be honest, I often invite people to ask their fellow participants, "How would you describe my *being*?" They share the perceptions that they've built over the short period of that programme, and they can be surprising.

How, then, does your actual *being* relate to the vision you have created of how you want to be regarded as a leader – whether in HR or not? Once you are clear about this, you can work out the building blocks of how to achieve your desired impression. For the vast majority of the leaders I work with, there is nothing manipulative about this – they don't want to come across as something they're not, but rather to be true to their real self.

We all develop patterns of behaviour – a kind of default – that can cease to serve us well. Our brains love to save energy by putting things into a 'I don't need to think about this any more, just do it' category. Yet how we come across needs to be at front of mind because it is so vital to the results that can be delivered.

By taking an honest and deep look at those practices, and the beliefs that underpin them, leaders can move to a higher level of authenticity. It often takes a period of discomfort to get there, as you try out different behaviours and don't always get the results you want immediately. We have to remember that we are 'retraining' our audience to expect something different, as well as retraining ourselves. This is how we manage our reputation.

It is extremely helpful for leaders to check out their beliefs at the most fundamental level. What are your beliefs about yourself? What are you telling yourself, in a difficult moment or before an important meeting? How supportive, or kind, are you to yourself? This reflection can reveal whether you are supported by positive beliefs that enable you to access your best resources or are allowing negative beliefs into your subconscious, which can undermine your confidence.

Corporate life can create an environment that feels rather unsympathetic, but in my experience, it is often the case that this is an interpretation rather than a fact. Everyone else seems to look as though they are strong, confident, dynamic and without any self-doubt. From my experience as a coach, I can reveal that this is absolutely not true. There is a vulnerable child inside all of us; it is part of the human condition.

We have explored three dimensions in terms of reputation: the HR function, the HR leader or professional, and the human being. In an ideal world, the narrative for all three would be completely aligned. For example, at all three levels you would probably be comfortable with words such as 'business-savvy', 'credible' or 'proactive'.

It is a vital first stage to become clear about how you would like to be described. Then you can put actions in place to turn that into reality. Let's look now at how you can *create*, *predict* and *respond to* the occasions when people build up this impression of you.

Identify the moments that matter

When are the opportunities for you to consciously build your reputation? You probably already have a diary full of meetings, and the secret is to work out where, and when, you can start to introduce your new, or revised, messages and behavioural approaches.

First, we will explore the moments that you can *create* – proactively decide to create an opportunity to progress your own agenda.

One of the most successful things I ever did as an HR director was to go around the countries in my client group and explain what HR did. This arose from the most stressful challenge I'd faced in my HR career. The vice-president for HR had masterminded a global corporate restructuring into a matrix structure, from her ivory tower in New York and, in addition to being required to implement the restructuring for Europe, I was told, "You no longer have an automatic seat at the table. You have to earn it."

It was a hard message to hear and threw me into a spin. However, in retrospect, this was the period in my career where I absolutely learned the most. The truth is, most people don't really understand what HR does, and I took a presentation on a roadshow across Europe that opened up exciting new conversations and a much more cohesive HR strategy.

Second, there are the moments that you can *predict*.

Some you can see coming up, such as corporate events or major meetings. Some happen regularly, such as the budget planning process, the weekly management meeting, your one-to-one with your boss or a line manager coming to you for advice. As an exercise to build your self-awareness and understand how you may currently be coming across, think of one of these meetings in the recent past. We're going to look at how your mindset affected how you came across.

Imagine that you're a fly on the wall, and remember the things that you said, how you expressed yourself, your body language and how you felt. How did you 'turn up' to that meeting? For example, was your mindset to act as a coach or facilitator of others' thinking, or were you pushing or defending a project or position, or were you feeling that your role was to advise? How conscious were you of your mindset at the time?

Then, consciously analyse how your mindset may have driven your behaviours. To what extent do you feel you came across as you would wish? What could you have changed to alter the outcome?

Finally, there are those moments that you can *respond to*.

These are the occasions that you can't predict – such as meeting someone in the corridor, at the water cooler or in the informal chat before or after a meeting – but you can still be ready for them

Imagine the power you can build by using all these opportunities to demonstrate, consciously and consistently, all the elements of message, tone and behaviour that will build your desired reputation.

Reputation provides the power you need to achieve your goals

In my experience, HR people are modest and shouting about their achievements does not sit comfortably with them. However, let's consider this question: if you had the power to do anything, as an HR function, what great things would you do?

Reputation opens doors and earns a seat at the table where decisions are made. When HR has a strong reputation, you get stronger people outcomes. It's worth working on.

Where should you put building reputation into your planning? Do you think about reputation after the event, when you're ready to talk about the results of the great work you've done? As any public relations (PR) specialist knows, we should think about it right at the beginning if we want our event, or intervention, to have maximum impact. We can then manage every step with our antennae out for every PR opportunity as well as pre-planning how we want it to be seen.

Because HR achieves little without others, the way it engages with and involves people is also critical to its reputation. In my European HR role, I often had to 'roll out' interventions designed by our US head office. Typically, these were appropriate for the US, but not for every European market. As well as wasting resources, these interventions were damaging to HR's reputation. They showed a lack of understanding of the real challenges facing the leaders in those markets, and no dialogue about them was available. They were finished to a high level of completeness before anyone outside the US was aware, never mind consulted.

There is no power in that. It may have felt powerful, being able to 'roll out' interventions across the world. The feeling of power was probably intellectual as well as influential – the initiatives themselves were best practice, and brilliant in the eyes of HR professionals. They would have made a great presentation at an HR networking event.

But they weren't fit for purpose and therefore would not achieve the optimum ROI. We will talk more about this in Chapter 10, which looks at **Focus**. For my part, during those episodes I felt completely torn – between supporting my HR hierarchy and looking as though I didn't understand reality. I understood both sides.

So, where *is* the power? How do we build it, and not throw it away as in this example? How do we use it wisely? One simple answer is to say that power lies in relationships, and in harnessing that power in a cohesive way across the organisation.

HR can build power through processes as well as behaviour. That can, however, be an ethical minefield. There is a risk to relationships when HR processes are known to be part of decisions that are made behind closed doors, for example, whether people are seen as future talent – or not.

I was conducting a leadership programme for a global company involving participants from different functions as well as countries, when the first session felt much stickier than usual – people weren't speaking up. During the break, a participant grabbed me and shared his impassioned thoughts about one of the points we'd been discussing. "Why didn't you share your thoughts during the session?" I asked, "I think others would have benefited." He checked that no one was listening before he said, "HR is in the room."

It is true that HR people are extremely powerful in that organisation, and this is a delicate responsibility. I had envied it, until that point. Their power did give them high levels of cooperation across the business, and HR people were in all the key meetings. However, the company was known to 'lose' the bottom 10% of performers every year too, and HR was seen as complicit in that rather uncompromising policy.

This wasn't fair to the HR people in that leadership programme, and I brought into the open what the participant had said. HR people are human too; they were there for their own development and needed to feel able to share their own challenges and vulnerabilities. It provoked a discussion that was valuable for all involved.

HR as a function does benefit from organisational power, especially for compliance and governance. By contrast, good HR people are often also valued for their compassion. Those two dimensions are not easy bedfellows, and this is where advocacy is such a useful technique – to explain, and reinforce, the dilemmas that HR has to manage. It isn't a question of either/or, it's both/and. For example, it is important for HR people to be seen as supportive, *and also* for them to turn those conversations into positive business outcomes.

A great way to explore a question as complex as this is to say, "What we need to work out is, for example, how we can establish the right amount of influence so that HR can drive our people agenda, while also being the team people can turn to when they need help." What I like about this wording is that it's an inclusive question for the whole organisation – for business leaders as well as HR leaders. You could offer it to your leadership team to debate.

HR's power comes from this kind of alignment – ensuring that people across the business understand the business benefits of HR being trusted and approachable. It's a strength rather than a weakness, which enables the organisation to leverage people's talents.

Reputation opens doors

Reputation is like an asset, to be valued and protected. As mentioned earlier, reputation includes what people say about HR when its people aren't in the room. In your organisation, do people say, "We need to get HR involved right from the start; we need their help to work through all the people issues," or, "Let's not tell HR just yet; they'll put obstacles in the way"? It's easy to undermine HR, partly because it is exposed on so many fronts – the 'obstacles', for example, are often legislative or regulatory, but HR is the messenger that gets the bullet.

Ideally, HR people are already in the room. An HR director said to me recently, "I knew my credibility was established when the chief executive asked me to help him think something through. It was a business issue rather than an HR one." The people aspects of that business issue subsequently emerged from the discussion – but it was about business first, and that's where HR needs to be.

It's your reputation and credibility that get you into the room. If you're not in the room, you can't contribute or influence.

HR needs to be included when it matters. Yet how do we know when we're being excluded when it matters, if we're not there to work that out? HR is tuned into the people implications of every decision or issue in a way that others often won't be. It would be difficult to identify any subject where there weren't any people implications.

This is well understood by HR leaders. They've known it for decades, yet this battle for recognition is far from won. One valuable technique can be HR advocacy. HR can be far more transparent about what it does, and why. This became evident to me during the post-restructuring roadshow that I mentioned earlier. My audience would say to me, "I had no idea HR did all that." HR people are normally so busy that they don't see self-promotion as a priority and, of course, there is much that they don't feel able to discuss.

Let's take the harassment example I used earlier. To advertise that you've had several discussions about this with leaders, and helped change their behaviour, would offer a mixed message. Although this may be good for HR's credibility, it's an example of where HR would want to mitigate the impact on the leader's reputation. For most HR professionals, respecting confidentiality and building the credibility of leaders will be more front of mind than blowing their own trumpet. In my own HR roles, I felt I'd done a good job when I'd helped a leader to look great. That helps everyone.

HR's reputation is built by being seen as an enabler. During a recent HR business partner programme, we continually reinforced the message that the business partners' priority is to help and support leaders. That role, and the spirit behind it, must be supported from the top down, by leaders in HR as well as in the business.

When important decisions are being made HR must be in the room. The people in the organisation need their interests, development and careers to be represented, as well as sound values and integrity. HR's role is to champion the people agenda, for everyone's sake, and it must build a platform from which to achieve this. Being in the right place, at the right time, with the right level of influence, is a critical ingredient. We can call this political intelligence, and will look more deeply at this shortly. Later in the book, we will look at how to make the most of these opportunities through relationships.

Make sure HR gets the credit (not the blame)

Credit where it's due, and blame where it's due. This conundrum can be a bit like a doctor-patient relationship, where a sick patient becomes resentful of the doctor and the treatment that they recommend. It all gets mixed up – the illness and the cure, especially when the cure is inconvenient or painful.

Think of a recent HR initiative. What did people say about it? To what extent was it embraced? Let's take the example of training for managers, say, coaching skills. This is a classic intervention to improve the retention and development of team members – helping them to perform better, enjoy their work more, feel supported, develop to the next level and stay.

The manager receives her invitation from HR (or L&D: we'll assume they're part of HR) but it's a really busy time. The manager asks her boss about it, and the boss says they're all just too busy and she can't go. As someone who runs many programmes, I know this happens all the time – two or three people don't turn up, the opportunity for them is lost and the money is wasted.

In that moment, the manager's boss had to decide about what was most important, and they chose operational pressure. We could say it's like Stephen Covey's 'urgent' versus 'important'. The reputation of HR, its initiative and how it communicated this, was a key factor in that wasteful decision.

Another typical example is that of applying performance ratings. Recently I worked with an organisation to help it build the integrity of its ratings – there had been an upward drift, with too many A and B ratings given, so we ran some short workshops.

Allocating pay awards within performance-related pay is a budgeting issue, with managers needing to allocate their budget fairly. However, the process is run by HR. Many managers want to give decent pay rises to team members, and for good reason. Budgets – their own budgets – mean that they can't. HR's role in this is to ensure that the process is used consistently, which drives fairness across the organisation. HR gets caught in the crossfire and must explain clearly the distinction between the a) ownership of the process and b) ownership of the decision.

In my own HR roles, I recall one manager who believed that a low rating motivated people to do better, while another believed a high rating to be motivating. Without going into whether either of these opinions are valid, it isn't fair for someone's pay award to be based on either of them. This was the central challenge of our workshop – getting everyone back on the same page, seeing fairness clearly after a period of blurring.

Make the true ownership transparent

Organisations can achieve more transparency in the relationship between HR and line leaders and managers. In my example, HR owned the process and probably the spirit behind the process – of fairness within a transparent structure. The line leaders and managers own the responsibility to be objective about performance, and to develop it.

Our workshop included techniques for coaching, giving feedback and challenging poor performance, and it is those activities that drive improved performance, rather than the rating itself. The process forces the issue, in a way that can be awkward and inconvenient; once a year, the manager's true opinion of a team member's performance comes into sharp focus and they should be held fully accountable for it. They have to own it, with their team member, as well as with their own boss.

Building this transparency is key to HR's reputation and can be used to its advantage, strategically and operationally. Business leaders shouldn't let people get away with saying, "I wanted to give you a higher rating, but HR wouldn't let me."

Building HR's reputation includes getting these messages to be communicated by business leaders. This may involve providing key phrases, for example, in the wording in regular communications from leaders about the performance management process, and the spirit and values that underpin it.

Organisations need to remove the fuel that can be used to undermine HR. It is in no one's interests. HR can make an easy and convenient scapegoat, when in fact its people are the agents of leaders. They apply their specialist expertise, insights and experience to the various challenges brought by today's world and the challenges their organisation faces. There may be some baggage; current incumbents may have inherited a lower reputation than they deserve. Whatever HR's basepoint, there are many ways to drive its reputation positively, in a way which gives it more power to do its work in the organisation.

Professional credibility is built on results

People need to trust HR's judgment. This will be built over time, as its judgment is tested — as a function and as individual professionals. Sometimes, counter-intuitively, this is achieved when a line manager refuses to accept advice or fails to run a conversation in the way they were advised to, for example, in a meeting about performance. They then have to face the consequences; a boss of mine used to call this a 'teachable moment'. He was very clear – set out the options and let them decide.

On one occasion, a clinical director in our pharmaceutical business lost a regulatory manager, in a niche specialism for which it was tough to recruit. We managed to replace him, with great difficulty, but I subsequently heard the same story from the newly-appointed manager about the director's same inept treatment. I tried coaching the director and facilitating meetings between the two, but his arrogance – intellectual, I think; he was a revered expert in his area – just got in the way.

I felt personally responsible when the manager inevitably resigned, but fortunately my boss helped me distinguish between what I was responsible for, and what I wasn't. "You can lead a horse to water, but you can't make it drink." Thankfully, the director did learn his lesson and we moved forward more constructively. He also counselled others to listen to my advice.

A key element here was that my HR director had a strong relationship with his boss, the chief executive, and with the clinical director's boss, the medical director. We worked together to solve this problem, in our different ways, and trusted one another. It strengthened my courage, knowing that they would understand and that the responsibility would be shared. I knew they would support me when I was not in the room – it would not damage my reputation.

HR is quite a technical area: there is much to learn in order to feel professionally credible. Mastery can be a key driver for HR professionals and careers can take many shapes. For example, starting off in HR you are often in administration, which may involve law, regulations and policy; or you may work in recruitment, talent or reward; or learning and development. There is so much to explore in all these areas: HR people are expected to be experts, and these specialisms now offer great depth. On the other hand, many HR people, like me, operate as generalists and seek to have some understanding of all the specialisms so that they can relate them to their client groups.

This is the concept of centres of expertise and HR business partners in action. The centres of expertise build their specialist knowledge so that they can bring the very best and latest thinking to their organisations. The HR business partner's role is to work from the other end, to understand what is required operationally. The quality of the dialogue between these different HR teams is also critical to HR's credibility. The centres of expertise offer mastery of their topic, and the HR business partners offer insight into the client groups, as well as having the relationships in place through which interventions can be implemented.

Mastery and judgment are not the same thing. In my earlier example of the roll-out of the US intervention, I believe that mastery got the better of judgment – it was an elegant solution but ill-judged in its implementation. HR will not, sadly, build credibility or reputation from the sophistication or elegance of its interventions, but from the appropriateness. Less is often more, but much harder to achieve.

Some of the most successful initiatives work because they have been stripped down to their basic elements. In a retail and leisure organisation, I was involved in a major restructuring and rethink of values and strategy. We did some engagement research and managed to boil the values down to three: around honesty, teamwork and striving to improve. Because these values suited the culture, they slipped easily into their language and into new ways of working. They wouldn't have won any awards for sophistication, but we were proud of the contribution they made to the culture of the new organisation.

Credibility and reputation come from results. It can be difficult for HR to isolate its own contribution to results because, as I mentioned earlier, it achieves through others and can be several steps removed from the front line. We will look later, in our chapter about **Focus** (Chapter 10), at how HR can prove its ROI. For some there are hard numbers that can be allocated to specific teams or people, such as vacancies filled or attendance on training courses. Others are shared measures, such as engagement or retention.

Given the complexity of achieving clear-cut ways of measuring HR's contribution, one approach is to measure the activities that are the enablers of results. We will explore this later in our chapter about **Rigour** (Chapter 9). Reputation is one enabler of HR's ability to deliver what the organisation needs. The quality of HR's relationships is another, and they work together.

I saw this in action when running a roadshow of short workshops for a client. In her own location, we had high attendance, meaning that the cost per trainee for that session was low. In a different location, the attendance was so low that the training proved expensive per trainee. The poor quality of the relationship undermined the intervention. Clearly, she was able to build good relationships, but hadn't sufficiently invested in this in the other location.

HR teams, like any other, need to be able to get feedback on how they are regarded. We can measure the quality of HR's relationships with stakeholders and obtain feedback that enables even stronger relationships to develop. Can we measure credibility and therefore reputation? As it is an enabler of HR's ability to deliver results, we must.

Here's one way to elicit personal feedback in a simple way, without an evaluation form or clever technology. For the process to be constructive, it's important that the recipient themself invites the feedback, from people they select. For example, simply ask for feedback in an email, with some suitable positioning that comes from the heart:

> It is very important to me that we work well together, so I would value your honest feedback. Please answer these two questions and provide any examples that illustrate your feedback:
>
> 1. When I am operating at my best, what is it that you see me doing?
>
> 2. When I am not demonstrating my full potential, what is it that you see me doing?'

You can see that this would open a valuable discussion about how the recipient is regarded, in terms of their credibility and other factors. A further question may be added to either question, or both, and works well in the follow-up conversation:

> What was the impact of this?

This gets us closer to working out the actual contribution of this HR person and helps the HR team gather anecdotes and stories that illustrate their value and build HR's reputation.

Learning from feedback helps HR to understand what its reputation is built on, and how to do more of that. It is vitally important for

HR to celebrate its achievements, and this means first clarifying them. Pride is important for any professional, and in HR it can be harder to come by if reputational factors are not proactively managed. Reputation comes at the beginning and at the end of any cycle and must be constantly kept in mind.

Here are some questions for you to consider:

- What do you want HR to be known for?

- What is standing in the way of that, or doing even more of that?

- Where does pride come from for you?

- What do you, personally, want to be known for?

- When are the opportunities that you could *create, predict* or *respond to*, to build your reputation?

CHAPTER 5

Connection

Making and nurturing the right connections across the business to help HR to target and deliver services in the most effective way possible; earning a seat at the table; political savvy.

If you're not invited, you can't contribute. That's the purpose of connection. HR can get pushed into the process role. Raising the level and quality of HR's relationships delivers greater profitability.

There is a whole science around how organisations can be structured – but in reality, it's all about relationships. The major trend in recent decades has been away from traditional hierarchy and towards what's loosely termed 'matrix'. Initially, organisational structures could be drawn as a two-dimensional matrix (for example, with product categories across the top and geographical regions down the side), then like a cube (for example, to add market sector). In many organisations today, the complexity of their structures has gone beyond our ability to draw them and, quite often, clients are unable to provide an organisation chart for me when I work with them. Reporting lines have ceased to have the same importance; roles are far more fluid, and everything changes constantly.

Today, organisations are held together by relationships. Individual leaders and managers are given goals and accountabilities, and often have to work out *how* for themselves. This can feel a lot less comfortable than being given direction, but it does enable people to create their own niche. This is why coaching is so important and popular today: it provides a supportive environment for leaders to work out how they want to operate; how to build influence and credibility in their role; and how to nurture relationships. There is so much uniqueness in roles today, and therefore much to navigate.

It is also vital to understand the political landscape of your organisation – how power works, whose support you need and the obstacles you could encounter. In this chapter, therefore, we move between the big picture of the stakeholder environment and the one-to-one interactions that count. Let's begin at the human level.

Trust delivers better outcomes

Neuroscience is providing us with fresh insights into how our brains work, and how our intellect interacts with our emotions. The technology of moving imaging has illuminated how our brains fire up in different areas and trigger physical as well as behavioural responses. The more primitive parts of our brains exert instant power over us with a voice that is inarticulate and difficult to resist.

We are not as controlled or as rational as we like to think, and this affects every interaction. We filter what we experience through our own unique lens, built from many sources: our experiences, beliefs, personality and how we are feeling about ourselves on any particular day.

This science has helped us to understand fully the vital importance of trust. We are allowing the masks we wear in corporate life to become more and more transparent – for the right reasons. Intellectually, we now understand that we operate at a higher level if we can be our true selves. Neuroscience has shown us how psychological safety releases the power of our brains, and so organisations are redesigning themselves, and developing their leaders, to reduce fear rather than use fear. For example, many leadership programmes now include a focus on emotional intelligence, authentic leadership and building trust, and pay structures reward the required behaviours as well as results.

Honesty supports problem-solving and innovation, both of which are vital in organisations. Feeling safe helps us to say what we really think.

Organisations need HR to be the honest arbiter. This can be easier for a consultant than for an internal HR director. In two client organisations, I needed to help the respective chief executives to face up to the fact that one of their director's performance was inadequate. At that level, it's too important to ignore, but a tough message to give and to hear. They knew it already, of course, but a busy chief executive is likely to hope that things will get better.

Being able to speak the truth, and talk about what matters, separates the organisations that do well despite challenging times, and those that don't. Robust discussions and speed of decisions are critical factors when things get tough. Making sure that those decisions are the right ones, and that they have taken into account the input of the best brains, is where an environment of trust plays a vital role.

Consider a recent meeting where you were involved in making an important decision. How safe did you feel to say what you truly thought? What percentage of your appropriate thoughts did you share? How much care and diplomacy did you feel you had to put into how you positioned your input? This is where neuroscience has taught us so much – we have only so much energy in our brains, and if you're using it on your careful positioning (which has an element of fear in it, thus triggering the amygdala), you can't use that energy intellectually. Your brain can't be in top gear.

Building trust in connections

We're learning to be much more honest about our feelings too – to bring them out into the open. This can help us on our journey to build trust.

Think of a recent meeting where you felt frustrated – perhaps:

a. progress was too slow; or

b. you felt there was a hidden agenda; or

c. you wanted more time to think

These are all valid responses – the frustration was part emotional, part rational. If we seek to understand our responses, we can neutralise the frustration. If we don't manage frustration, the danger is that we *become* our frustration – we all know what that looks and feels like.

Here's a technique to use. Quite simply, have a quick chat with your frustration. I have a theory (unproven) that our frustration is telling us that we have a need that isn't being met. Let's use the examples above:

a. Progress was too slow – your need is to make more happen. We have the option to speak it out, for example, "What's worrying me is that I [or we] have a deadline, and

I'd hoped to make more progress in this meeting." Whether you manage to fix the speed of progress or not, you instantly feel better.

b. The hidden agenda feeling – your need is for openness. Trust takes time to develop. While you make a mental note to do some work on the trust between you, you can state in the moment, "I feel that we're not quite on the same page. I think it would help us both if we share what we'd really like to get from this meeting."

c. Wanting more time to think – your need is likely to be for correctness, to get the right decision. You may also have the introversion preference and need space to think clearly. This is entirely reasonable, and you can state it, "I just need to reflect for a short time, and I'll get back to you." Agree when, and make sure that you do.

Sharing our emotions helps to build trust; we value it in others and that gives us more courage to do it ourselves. Only then can we share what we really think: concerns and doubts as well as positive inputs such as ideas and optimism.

Building trust can be hard work, largely because of the conflict that's inherent in organisations. Imagine a typical management meeting, with people around the table representing sales, marketing, finance, IT, customer service, product quality, risk, and so forth, as well as HR. We actually need this conflict, so that we work out the best solutions for all our stakeholders as well as for the bottom line. This is why the matrix structure was invented – to make these wholly legitimate conflicts explicit, and make people tackle them head-on.

There has been much research done about trust. There are four factors that emerge consistently:

1. **Competence or capability** – the belief that the person can do the particular work. You may trust your friend to drive you to the airport, for example, but not to pilot the plane.

2. **Reliability** – whether they do what they say they're going to do; keep their promises; deliver on time.

3. **Familiarity or intimacy** – this is about how well you know them; the feeling you get when someone is predictable and you know what to expect; they're consistent, even if they're irritating. You don't have to like them, but it helps.

4. **Their commitment to you** – the evidence, or feeling, that they're on your side; will back you up and advocate for you.

This is a useful framework to evaluate the level of trust you have with someone, and why. Think of a key stakeholder. Taking each of these four areas in turn, score the person high, medium or low. This can help you to pinpoint how to build more trust.

Naturally, this evaluation of trust goes both ways. Others will be assessing to what level they trust you too. It's most often done instinctively and subconsciously, as we decide who we think is in our tribe.

Trust can be difficult to achieve when there are so many conflicting agendas in organisations. Conflict may seem personal, but it rarely is. It helps to neutralise conflict when you bear this in mind.

A credible influencer – in the moment

Our research, as well as our experience, proves that there are some interactions that are pivotal in achieving your goals – the moments that matter, which we explored in the previous chapter. Some you have planned for, and some take you by surprise. However they came about, only you can make the most of the moment. You can't relive it (except in your mind, of course, when you think of what you could have said). The power is in the moment.

This graphic gives us an overarching process – a strategy that can be built to give real clarity to individual interactions:

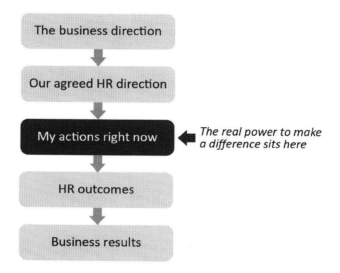

In this chapter about connection, we recognise that credibility and influence are built over time, conversation by conversation. We need a strategy for it, as a function and as individuals. Then we can leverage the moments that matter.

In Chapter 2 we talked about the organisation's strategic narrative, and how HR's own story can fit within that. However, all that work can be lost in a moment. If what we say, and the way we say it, is not aligned with how we want to come across, the opportunity is lost.

Working with a market data company some years ago, I heard an excellent example of this. They were undertaking a substantial restructuring of just about everything – IT platform, organisation, people, systems – so that they could operate as globally as their major clients. I was invited to their kick-off session so that I would fully understand what they were doing and give informed and aligned messages in the communication skills programmes I was running for them.

I was impressed. It had all been thought through thoroughly, the presentation itself was snazzy and the speakers were well-rehearsed and looking confident. I said this to the participants in my first session, and one said, "I thought so too, until I saw one of the directors in the corridor afterwards. He said, 'Yes, looked good, didn't it, but we've heard it all before, haven't we?'" All that hard work and polish had been completely undone in a casual sigh. The credibility of the whole programme, as well as that of the individual director, was thrown away recklessly.

Does this mean we've got to be 'on' all the time? I'm afraid so. As I said earlier, we are being watched all the time. But we can learn to master our personal behaviours in a way that is congruent with who we are as a person as well as a leader. Being your authentic self is also less stressful. Being a credible influencer in the moment can be built on your own true values, and we will explore this later in Chapter 7, which looks at **Balance**.

To be convincing, we need to prepare key messages in advance. We need to be consistent and repeat them. We tend to worry too much about repeating ourselves. I once heard a comms specialist say, "People start to really hear something only when we're sick of saying it." The term 'elevator pitch' is rather dated, but people do seem to still understand the need to have a message – consciously chosen and crafted – at front of mind at all times, so that it slips easily out of the mouth.

In my HR team we used to say – and think to ourselves, to guide our behaviour – "We want to be partners in the business." It was a relatively new concept then, and it really helped us to move conversations in the right direction and use the right questions. For example, we could say to a sales director, "Our role is to be partners with you in getting what you need from your people. What's bothering you right now in terms of their performance?"

You may be in a situation right now where you know your stakeholders well, and feel you are beyond the point of making clear what you want to offer in your relationship with them. My aim with this book is to enable HR and business leaders to work more productively together, and this means moving the relationship forward rather than being content with where it is now. Challenge is key in today's organisations. When we nurture deep connections, we enable everyone to share all their talents.

Think of a meeting coming up, with a key stakeholder. You probably have some knowledge of what's expected of you. In this moment, with them, how could you offer more? What could add even more value? The only way to get there is to explore *their* world. What's happening, for them, that you can tune into?

Being a credible influencer in the moment means being fully conscious of who you are and what you offer. This provides a firm foundation to reach out and explore the other person's needs.

Being credible in today's organisations demands that you demonstrate that you understand that conflict. In later chapters (in particular, Chapter 6 on **Perspective**), we will explore the data and other inputs that you can bring into meetings, to demonstrate that you're on top of reality. In this chapter, we're looking at how you do that *behaviourally*.

First, we have to be fully present. When you are in a meeting, it's all too easy to be preoccupied – by the meeting you've just had, the meeting that's next, or the email you've just had from your boss. Being fully present in the meeting you're in, right now, demands your full attention. Allowing yourself to be distracted dilutes your power, in this moment, and this moment is pivotal to what happens next.

If you are not fully present, you cannot become fully connected in the way you need to be if you are going to build this relationship. Being fully present requires bringing your whole self to the conversation: your emotional self as well as your professional self.

Being a credible influencer starts here. People know whether you are in the room with them, in spirit as well as in body. Let's look next at marshalling the spirit that will get you the result that you want.

Clarify your intent

How will you 'turn up' to a meeting? For example, will your intent be to solve problems, give expert advice, or coach? You may move between these, consciously or automatically. What is your default intent? It may be the subject of the meeting that will dictate your intent, for example, a difficult disciplinary situation with a manager who seems to get into trouble often, or a meeting with a colleague who you get on well with and will enjoy developing ideas together.

Some people seem to have a rather fixed intent, that is, driven by how they see themselves and their value in their world. I have a friend who always seems to feel she should give an answer, and I know her intent is good, but her mode seems rather stuck on that of expert adviser. It's her default, and she finds it comfortable. The set of behaviours are well practised – a kind of groove.

There's some fascinating neuroscience to support this: neural pathways. Our brains much prefer to repeat actions rather than to devise new ones; as I mentioned earlier, brains love to save energy. This is why challenging old habits is hard work, and training ourselves in new routines takes discipline. It is proven that we can control our thoughts, which is both exciting and scary. It's also another reason to repeat our key messages – to 'programme' ourselves as well as our stakeholders to see us as we want to be seen.

Building productive relationships can be as much about what we don't say as what we do. It means knowing when to listen, and how to phrase a question so that it helps others to think. Our intent will 'leak' into the question, for example, when using a leading question that contains the answer we want. A truly open question is one that invites the person to expand their own thinking about their problem.

Coaching is core to the value that you, as an HR director, add to your leadership team. The ability to ask a question that opens options is highly valued. Whether it's about a challenging conversation that's coming up, an important presentation or an operational issue, a great place to start is to ask, "How would you like this to turn out?" From this question, you then hear the person work out how to achieve that. Once they become clear about what they want, the rest falls into place. We feel blocked when we're not clear.

The reward you earn from asking open, powerful questions is that you are much better prepared to influence effectively. You get more material to work with, and you create openness. You create a climate in which your own input will be welcomed, and you can share those elements of your insight that are entirely relevant to what you discover. You can position your own aims, project or issue with more sensitivity to the other person's needs or way of seeing the world.

Winning a seat at the table – political intelligence

We are political animals. I've often heard it said, "HR shouldn't be political," or (from HR people themselves), "I don't do politics – I keep out of it." This is, in fact, a political position – it's the strategy of being passive. Being intentionally passive is rarely effective.

It is indeed tricky for HR to 'get into' organisational politics – there are real risks to HR's reputation as honest brokers, arbiters of fairness and upholders of values. However, HR can just as easily get caught out by using the avoidance strategy. People draw conclusions about why you stay out of something, just as they judge your actions if you get stuck in.

The solution is to build a proactive and positive political strategy so that you build the connections and the credibility that ensure you get a seat at the table when it matters.

There are good reasons for HR to become smart at politics, and this can be achieved with its integrity intact. HR needs to be at that table, for the good of everyone. The people agenda needs to be represented, and people are a factor in just about every decision at every table. The real benefit from being politically intelligent is to be involved early. So often I hear from HR people that they should have been involved at an earlier stage, to share their insights around what can be resourced, for example, or the implications for roles or ways of working.

When HR is involved early, it can add maximum value. When HR is excluded, the impact can be costly to the organisation as well as frustrating for HR: it gets stuck with implementing something that could have been done so much better if they'd been able to influence it earlier.

So, let's look at how to develop a positive political strategy that sits comfortably with you, personally.

1. Build your stakeholder map

A good place to start is to consider the landscape of your organisation and build a map of your stakeholders.

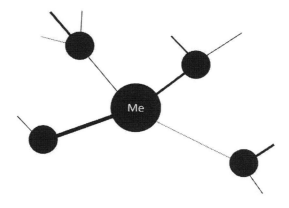

How important is each stakeholder to you in achieving your goals? Use the thickness of the line between you and them to indicate that – a bold line means they're very important, and a thin line means they're less important. Your boss should be included.

2. Evaluate your stakeholder relationships

Pick your top five stakeholder relationships, and consider the *sufficiency* of that relationship, that is, to what extent:

- you're on the same page – you understand each other

- they deliver – they don't let you down

- they help you reach your goals

- you trust them to represent you fairly

As you can see, this isn't about whether you like them, whether they're the person you like to chat with at the water cooler or have lunch with. Your trust evaluation from earlier will be useful in this. However, that was about the feeling of trust – and this is a tougher assessment of whether or not they help you to achieve the results you need.

Is the relationship sufficient or not? If you're not sure, or you don't know them well, then it is insufficient, and there's work to do.

Let's go back to my earlier example, with Erik in Frankfurt and Antonio in Rome, about rolling out my competency framework. In retrospect, my relationship with Erik was more sufficient that that with Antonio. Erik said, "No," but he told me the truth so that I knew where I stood. It was uncomfortable at the time, but straightforward. On the other hand, it was a much happier meeting with Antonio, who waved me off at the airport under the illusion that he was on board. Unfortunately, it was my boss who learned that Antonio wasn't doing as he'd promised, which made it embarrassing as well as disappointing. My relationship with Antonio, despite friendly lunches, proved to be insufficient.

3. Decide what or who you need to work on

Much of this book is about the actions you can take to improve relationships – your overall credibility and influence are core to your stature. In this section on political intelligence, let's take a step back and consider how power works.

A classic example used in leadership programmes is the budget-setting process. Leaders are often given a target that they don't agree with. Initially they see limited options; they'll say, "If I tell my boss we can't do it, that's bad for my career. So, what do I tell my team? Pretend I think we can do it when they know we can't, or tell them I don't agree with it either?" These are both passive options, because they are not tackling the issue at source. Sometimes the leader will say they've spoken to their boss, and their boss isn't tackling it either – they're also just swallowing realistic targets such as 'double-digit growth' because it's the aim across the organisation.

This is a good example of the strategic importance of political intelligence. I was with a highly respected, global organisation on the day it issued its first profits warning in 200 years. There's only one thing worse to analysts than not being successful, and that's not knowing what your own business can deliver. Having to give a profits warning is the end result of tiers of management accepting targets that are not achievable – if people had been honest and pushed back, the targets would have been more realistic, and the damage limited.

Building credibility with your most important stakeholders is the most critical part of political intelligence. This is likely to include your boss, your boss's boss and other senior people whose respect you need. You need them to believe you when you speak, and to trust your judgment.

The key elements of this are factors in several of our enablers. For example, in the section about **Focus** (Chapter 10), we will talk about the importance of using credible data, and in the section about **Push** (Chapter 8) we will talk about standing firm; so we will continue to work on building political intelligence in later chapters.

We lead through relationships

We manage through meetings, but it's the depth of our connections that enables us to lead. In meetings, we go through action points, project progress and workstreams. In meetings, we are most often operating within a framework that has already been set. I'm often surprised – and disappointed – to see how many meeting agendas don't include the real priorities.

When we make good progress in meetings, it is because good relationships are already in place, and this is often done outside the room. That's also how we influence the agenda.

When we allow our diaries to be filled with meetings, often slotted into our calendar by our colleagues or team members, we may not be leaving enough time to build those relationships that will open doors for us. Our boss's boss, for example, won't often come to us for a meeting: we have to go to them. They will probably welcome it when we do, but they won't initiate it. There may be crucial moments, however, when you need your boss's boss's support, and they need to respect your credibility.

Building this framework for influence never seems an urgent priority. It tends to smack us in the face when it's too late – the spreadsheet needs to be signed off. You've been so busy delivering this year's targets, it's understandable that you weren't thinking about how to manage the expectations for next year.

Let's go back to our target-setting issue. When you tell your boss that you don't feel the target you've been given is achievable, their immediate concern is how they're going to handle it with their own boss. The ideal scenario for all involved is that you've already achieved this credibility, personally, with them both.

Building leadership through relationships requires a plan – to nurture the strategic relationships that will help you to deliver results. This should cover all the parts of the organisation that can benefit from your input. I put it this way because, in one of my own HR roles, I had two divisional vice-presidents and I got on with one much better than the other. Let's call them Bob and David. Bob was a natural people person, led his people well and understood HR, so we would work together happily and comfortably. David, on the other hand, was difficult to work with. It was a struggle to get a meeting in his diary, to get access to his teams, and to get good work moving. In retrospect, I feel he lacked confidence.

Who needed my help more – Bob or David? Of course, Bob got a much larger percentage of my time than David, but that was the wrong way around. I was so busy, I felt I didn't have the time or energy to keep pushing on a heavy door, and it was disheartening.

I needed a strategy to build trust with David, so that we could lead together, as I did with Bob. Standing up at conferences together, or supporting each other at meetings, and those easy interchanges between HR and business leaders, demonstrate that people matter.

They put HR in a leading position. Bob considered me a full member of his management team.

I was able to hold Bob to account, too, for his leadership and management. It's much easier to provide feedback to a leader when it's about something you've both agreed is right. The HR professional can point out to a leader, skilfully, how an action could be interpreted, or how it actually landed. Bob was quite a fiery character, and I was able to help him do some damage limitation because I was so confident of his positive intent.

If I were able to turn back the clock to my own corporate life, I would invest far more energy in this: scope out the landscape, and make building deep, trusting relationships a priority. Plan it, diarise it, evaluate it, problem-solve, and confront it when a relationship isn't working. Connections deliver results. The results of these powerful relationships are successful outcomes, as well as being able to celebrate together too.

Here are some questions for you to reflect on:

- How does power work in your organisation?

- Whose support do you need to achieve your goals.

- Which connections could deliver better outcomes?

- In which relationships do you enjoy high levels of trust? Why is that?

- What is your default intent – expert adviser, problem-solver, facilitator or coach?

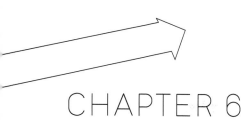

CHAPTER 6

Perspective

Taking a step back – systematically gathering and updating the information that enables HR to make robust decisions and engage others' support, developing insight and acting accordingly.

HR needs to show that it 'gets' the hard stuff – the business imperatives – as well as the people aspects of work. It's vital to take a step back and schedule some time to think about the context in which HR is operating and build deep insights into what drives success.

We all learn all the time, soaking up information, patterns and clues that can lead to some breakthrough thinking. Most importantly, HR can use its insight to demonstrate the value it adds.

In Chapter 5, about **Connection**, I explored how to nurture key relationships, which provide the best opportunities to learn. People tend to absorb and deal with what comes across their desk – but HR must not confine itself to HR. Relationships allow real exposure to how the organisation works; they open doors to the reality of business, to production lines and call centre operations as well as to important meetings.

One of the most valuable days in my HR career was spent travelling around with a pharmaceutical sales representative. Experiencing the front line and meeting some customers illuminated for me so many elements that are truly vital, and yet become overshadowed further up the line. The absolute purpose of my organisation was played out in front of me – the interface between the company and the customer, and the buying decision.

While travelling between calls, we chatted about his sales manager and how that relationship works, which taught me so much about the support salespeople need. As we all know, this doesn't mean that the best salesperson makes the best sales manager. While meeting the customer and witnessing the relationship the salesperson had so delicately built over a period, I more accurately understood the tension between meeting targets and protecting customer relationships.

I knew these things intellectually, but the day equipped me so much better to make the arguments, for example, pushing back against the top rep becoming the sales manager, and measuring sales reps purely on sales. It also gave me more credibility, to be able to say, "When I was with James at Kings Hospital, I could see that it was his ability to listen that built the relationship with the doctor – to judge whether or not to push for the sale right then."

This is the central purpose behind perspective – building, and being able to demonstrate, meaningful insight into what drives success so that HR's actions can be driven by that.

Understand the numbers

Every organisation has its own jargon for the numbers that matter – EBITDA, KPIs, etc. HR leaders need to use this language too, and understand what it means. Most organisations have priority indicators, and sometimes these are simplified into shorthand that everyone can understand. A telecoms company I worked with had one number (from 0 to 10) that was a formula combining two vital measures, for example, customer retention divided by monthly usage. Everyone knew the number every week and would say things like, "We're down 0.5 to 6.5 this month." They knew when they needed to act.

What are the priority numbers in your organisation? How quickly do they come to mind? Which acronyms are used most by business leaders? What do they really mean?

HR has a language of its own. Business leaders can be so switched off by HR jargon that they never get to learn what it really means. As in my example of the logistics finance director, if cost per mile is their favourite number, then that's where HR has to start.

Business acumen is key for HR leaders. There is a bit of an Equity card issue here – it's easier to learn this kind of dialogue, and how business leaders use it, if you're in the business or operational meetings. HR isn't always represented on the top board, and therefore it can be harder to get the opportunities to demonstrate this fluency. Whatever your level, get stuck in.

Here is a framework for thinking about how you can develop your business understanding and bring it into your conversations. You can see that this sets up a virtuous circle – the more you learn, the easier it is to talk about it, and thus you learn more.

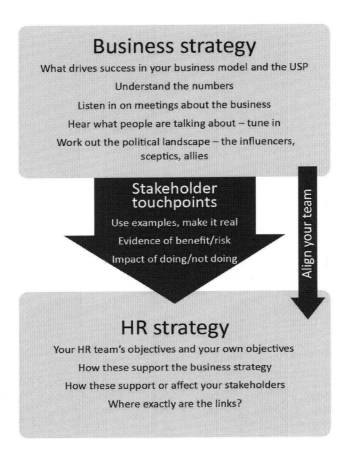

If this is something you would like to work on, there are more resources for you to build your business acumen on our website at https://www.enable-hr.com/perspective/business-acumen

The next stage is to use data to promote your HR agenda. This is quite difficult, simply because HR is more about enablers than outputs and these measures may not be readily available in your organisation. Usually, we need to make connections between hard and soft — we'll dig further into this in the next section.

People analytics is a field that's exploding, with data coming from all directions. Large organisations may have their own function, and some outsource it. However, HR must own HR data. The technology for continuous listening – gathering feedback more often across the employee lifecycle – is valuable, revealing and cost-effective. The key skill is to produce meaningful data and use it to create a compelling story.

What if you don't have this kind of data at your disposal right now? One way to illustrate the impact of, say, engagement, is to use the generic data provided by expert consultancies, which is generally updated every year and often related to different sectors and demographic groups. These reports and infographics often include compelling data that can have real impact for business leaders. For example, the top 20% performing companies may have engagement levels of 75% and that, therefore should be your target too.

Many senior leaders will be influenced by the numbers, which they will use to define their comfort zone. Using powerful data from respected organisations can help HR to make the discussion more strategic.

Sometimes we have to take several steps back when we have a difficult influencing challenge. There may be a basic concept to which we must have someone's buy-in before we can move on – and even help them to understand something they haven't thought about much before, such as engagement.

A former boss, my HR director, knew it would be a struggle to get our European vice-president on board with some leadership training. He took him out for a good lunch – those were the days – and came back looking delighted. "Did you get the budget?" I asked. "No," he said, "but I got him to use the word 'culture'." Every journey starts with the first step. Big lunches are out these days, but the HR director still needs to do their influencing one-to-one before key meetings.

A mix of financial illustrations and anecdotal evidence can be a powerful combination. HR tends to start with a small number, for example, "If we lose that manager, it will cost us six months' salary." This is informative, but it's the big numbers that get the board's attention. We can roll these numbers up into big totals that have real impact.

Understanding the enablers and the outcomes of success

This is a core challenge in demonstrating the ROI of HR. The analogy of the iceberg is useful here. The results that the business delivers are clearly above the waterline, as is what leaders and line managers do to produce the results – we can see it all happening. We can observe meetings and conversations, watch presentations and study spreadsheets – yet the quality of all that activity is driven by factors that are below the waterline.

Further down in the depths of our iceberg are many unseen activities and conversations that have a major impact on business results but are extremely difficult to measure. This is why we at Enable-HR decided that something that we could actually measure was the *quality* of the interaction between HR and the business, as explained in Chapter 3.

Here's an example that I am sure will be familiar to many HR leaders. I'll take you back to the company where our European vice-president had to be taught the word 'culture'. He wasn't a natural people person, to say the least, and many of his directors had real difficulty working for him. I spent a lot of time coaching them, smoothing their ruffled feathers and building their confidence for their next meeting with him. The cost and hassle of losing any of them would have been high and painful. This activity was invisible to him, but valuable as an enabler of their performance.

Incidentally, for me a great benefit of those conversations was learning how the business really worked at that level and, in our case, as part of a global organisation – they helped to build my perspective. The relationships driving the vice-president were those in the global headquarters, as they worked towards the benefits of economies of scale and brand consistency, for example. For his part, the vice-president was struggling to manage the conflicts stirred up by our European markets, and these were owned by the directors.

Is it valid for HR to say to the chief executive, "I just stopped that guy handing in his resignation – that will have saved us at least a year's salary, reputational damage and the impact on his team"? Yes, it is valid, but HR has to manage the trust element both ways – the director, most likely, will not want HR to tell the vice-president that they had a bad day. Conversations like this are carrying on every day in every organisation around the globe, where HR provides the oil that eases difficult situations.

A key difference between outputs and enablers is that the measures of outputs are most often retrospective – they tell you about what has just happened, in the past, for example, staff turnover. Enablers tell you about the strength of your organisation going forward, for example, the talent pipeline. This is why many organisations adopt the approach of the balanced scorecard. It's much more difficult to measure enablers, such as 'learning', which is a classic item on a balanced scorecard. However, if it's on there, people will be tasked to work out how to measure it. As we all know, what gets measured gets done.

See the Resources section for the work done by Dave Ulrich on the HR scorecard.

In one organisation, we had 'morale' on the scorecard. We did run engagement surveys, but wanted a more frequent, ongoing measure, even if it was subjective. So, we'd go around the table at the Monday board meeting and ask directors to give a score out of 10. This provoked a valuable conversation. For example, one director said, "Five," which was lower than the previous week. We asked him why, and he told a story of visits to several sites where people had seemed rather flat. Sales had in fact gone down, but for external reasons, and it was agreed to do something to give people a boost and reassure them that they weren't held responsible for the fall in sales. This rather vague measure provoked a valuable conversation around the table, and the next engagement results went up. Anecdotal evidence, impressions and intuition do have value, especially when subsequently checked out.

HR needs to know what drives success in their unique organisation. Every organisation has a unique business model. While I'm no financial expert, I did learn from one a remarkably simple way of looking at this many years ago. He explained that the cost structure needed to be built around a sustainable formula. For example, if you offer high levels of customer service then you will have to deliver that – allocate appropriate costs and maintain them because it's part of your brand. For example, Waitrose spends more money on customer service than Tesco does, and customers expect better service and shorter queues. Get to know your own organisation's business model and how it relates to that of competitors.

Let's return again to the finance director at the logistics company, whose favourite measure was the cost of vehicle usage. If getting goods delivered cheaply is the most important priority, this is fine. In practice, however, the company provided holistic logistic services for customers: it took a long time to win them, and then to integrate them, and building long-term relationships with them was vital. What was it that drove customer retention? Driver behaviour was key, as well as the customer relationship management provided by head office.

HR has to relate what they are doing to hard outcomes. We'll explore this in more depth when we look at **Focus** (Chapter 10). Here, in our chapter on **Perspective**, our aim is to build HR's insight into how their organisation works and what drives success. HR leaders need to soak up information, patterns and clues. These can be used in the moment, to demonstrate their understanding of what really matters, and also built into a more cohesive picture to make the case for investment in valuable interventions.

One area where data is generally being collected relates to the role of the line manager and the 'moments of truth' that matter to employees. The behaviour of line managers is now becoming more commonly accepted as a valid enabler of performance and therefore of productivity. It is often said that people leave managers, not companies. Continuous listening is an extremely valuable tool that allows companies to check out those critical moments along the employee journey. Examples could include evaluating how well a performance review went, or return to work after absence, or even a pulse survey on how well a team meeting went.

The external interface for employees

Organisations now appreciate the value of their employer brand, and how jobs are perceived externally. The pandemic, ironically, provided a recruitment boost to nurses, carers and refuse collectors. These jobs were seen to have real purpose, however tough. The way a product, service or vocation is seen has a direct impact on how eager people will be to apply for these jobs or develop these careers.

This is another reason why it's critical to understand how it all connects together. While working with a company producing cancer drugs, I struggled to understand what its highly technical job titles meant, but the company's purpose was clear. Saving lives is a compelling purpose that will pull in talent, and pharma companies use this to good advantage.

Building a reputation as a good employer is vital. It pays to remember that the best recruits are likely to have a choice, in the same way that the organisation wants to be able to choose the best applicants. Employees who recommend their employer are a valuable source of referrals. Websites such as Glassdoor capture these opinions, which of course can go both ways. There's nowhere to hide these days.

Viewing the employee as a customer is a valuable mindset – as an employer you're in a competitive situation too. Employees have a psychological contract with their employer that is easily broken, by their line manager or by a wider issue. HR needs to understand how to market internally, to employees, in the same way as the marketing function reaches out to customers. It pays to remember that employees – especially the most talented – also have a choice.

The chief executive relies on HR to provide insights into the external world – demographic, legislative and social trends. Demographics have come much more to the fore, especially as we experience differences between generations that are much more striking than ever. Changing attitudes towards work as well as technology mean that younger generations need to be treated differently. At first, it was thought that they would come to fit in, as earlier generations have ultimately tended to, but their preferences – for example, for flexibility – have aligned with other trends, including the use of technology and working from home.

It is the implications of these changes that HR needs to think through, in relation to the organisation's unique business model. How will they impact the organisation's ability to recruit the right talent, retain and develop them, and get reward right? This is where HR's specialist skills can be combined with real insight into the business and its people, to put the organisation in a strong position against its competitors. Building a competitive edge is just as important with internal customers as external. They will decide whether to work hard, remain loyal, or go elsewhere.

Build your perspective on how culture drives performance

Culture is the strategic remit of HR: it is critical to long-term success. This is where all the individual pieces of the jigsaw – the individual conversations, the behavioural training and the leadership workshops – come together into one big, beautiful picture.

Let's clarify what we mean by culture, so that we can look at it more deeply. There are various definitions, for example, "It's how we do things around here," or "It's how people solve problems." We can draw from the work done on understanding global cultures too – and this adds a further dimension. In one of my workshops on working cross-culturally, a participant came up with an original and insightful definition of culture. "Culture is as water to a fish," he said. A fish doesn't consciously feel water, in the same way as humans aren't conscious of the air around them. Culture can be like that – in a good way, or in a bad way.

Culture, too, has to start with the business imperatives. For example, if your organisation thrives on innovation, you need a culture that encourages and rewards experimentation and risk. On the other hand, if your business is in, say, aviation, your culture needs to be fundamentally risk-averse. You need both innovation and risk management in every organisation, but the balance between them will be different.

Charles Handy's familiar story held that if you put a frog into boiling water, it would jump straight out. If you put the frog into cool water and gradually heated it to boiling, it would die. The frog would accommodate the heat of the water until it couldn't any longer and would be cooked. Organisational cultures can be like that; people develop all kinds of coping strategies to deal with uncomfortable situations and feelings, but it can undermine their performance.

This is a tough area for HR to tackle – it can be like wrestling a blancmange. Because culture is made up of many people's individual actions, it has to be managed on many fronts. For example, when you ask a friend, "What's it like working at your company?" she may say, "It's great, I love the people and there's always a buzz," in which case there is quite a lot about the whole organisation in her response. If, on the other hand, she says, "I really get the chance to use my skills and I'm learning all the time," then her impression is more likely to be formed by the actions of her manager. Both are, in fact, a mix of individual, personal interactions with colleagues, managers and leaders, and of corporate interventions designed to stimulate the desired behaviours.

Culture has to start from the top. Getting senior leaders to invest their own energy and personal commitment is absolutely vital to any strategic cultural intervention. In addition, they, personally, have to live and be role models for it.

To make the case for this, senior leaders need to understand culture, how it impacts business performance, and how to drive the culture they need. This is why we are spending time on it in this chapter on perspective.

Let's take a classic example that many organisations have undertaken: moving towards a coaching culture. I was involved in such a programme with a major global bank. It had historically been focused on financial returns at every level; those who brought in the bucks were those who earned the bucks. There was a cost, though, in terms of disengagement and ability of staff to learn and flex in a sector that needed to change. The data proved that there were issues of retention and performance: the bank's culture was failing to create the right conditions to develop and retain talent.

There are many elements in a strategic intervention like this, from the 'hard' stuff of redesigning the pay structure (to reward behaviours as well as results), to the 'soft' stuff of learning how to build a much more developmental and supportive style of leadership and management. Managers developed their skills in coaching and giving feedback and were rewarded for those.

The strategic importance of the changes, and the business imperatives, were reinforced throughout all the programmes. All the jigsaw pieces needed to be carefully designed to fit together into the desired picture, to give consistent messages about how to treat people. Why and how this would lead to competitive advantage was made clear.

Data had been used to clarify the problem and its scope, to build the proposal, to track the intervention, and to measure success as it was embedded. This kind of data is indispensable when you're asking senior leaders to change their own behaviour.

Culture has to be driven from the top, especially the behavioural elements. Culture drives performance in so many ways. To simplify something that's very complex, culture shows people what is required of them. Those at the top must be role models for this.

For example, what do senior leaders talk about? What do they recognise and reward? What do they do when someone has tried something new and failed? How do they interact with people from lower levels? What opportunities do they create for more junior people to shine? These are powerful messages about what is valued, and HR needs to understand what actually happens in their organisation.

Business and HR leaders have to stand together and give the same messages, consistently and regularly. As HR people will know, many of these cultural messages are embedded in their policies, processes, interventions and learning workshops. The tone used in HR policies, for example, reveals a lot about how much trust is given to employees. Reading policies devised by organisations in different sectors can be surprising; for example, some ooze 'guilty until proven innocent', perhaps where theft or fraud are a major risk, while others can afford to be gentler in tone.

I worked for several years with a logistics organisation, where alongside our engagement survey and work with leaders, we were asked to investigate the issue of damage to customers' parcels. Although this was outside our usual remit, we spent the night observing and taking photos in the overnight distribution centre. It was a revelation. At one point, I saw a man standing on a customer's parcel. "Why are you standing on that?" I asked. "I need to reach to the top to get these other parcels in," he said. When I pointed out that he could find something else to stand on, rather than a customer's parcel, what became apparent was that no one had actually told him that it was important to look after customers' goods. There were many factors behind this, including a dictatorial leadership style. We identified many low-cost actions that could easily be taken, and some that took longer.

I started this chapter talking about a day with a sales rep and have concluded it with the tale of a night in a distribution centre. Both demonstrate that there is no substitute for HR people seeing for themselves how things work. Building HR's perspective of the full realities of their organisation – financial, commercial, managerial and behavioural – is critical. The example above is a good illustration of how the small pieces of the jigsaw build into the bigger picture.

Understanding that customers, and all their goods and interests, are the core of any organisation's success, seems so obvious as to not need saying. However, such 'obvious' realities sometimes need some digging out in order to build HR's deep insight into how the organisation works.

Building HR's full and complete perspective of your organisation enables you to speak the right language and to tackle the most important issues. Only when we understand reality can we make the best decisions about where to invest HR's resources.

Here are some questions for you to consider:

- What gets talked about most in your organisation?

- From whose perspective do you need to view a particular issue?

- How would you describe your existing culture? Ask some other people and consider to what extent this is supporting your business goals.

- What are the key enablers in your organisation – what drives success?

- How well aligned do your senior leaders and HR appear to be in the messages they give and how they act as role models for the required behaviours?

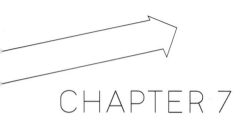

CHAPTER 7

Balance

This is about steering a path that values the needs of all stakeholders; developing approaches that stick; taking the long-term view while role modelling the organisation's values.

Building HR's understanding of how the whole organisation works is critical. The next stage is to learn about the interests of all the stakeholders involved and how they conflict. We talked earlier about the fact that conflict is inherent in organisations – indeed, it's designed in on purpose. For example, those responsible for the product may drive for high quality and consistency, while finance will want to keep costs down, and the sales team will want new products to sell. That's because the world outside is full of conflict and difference, and organisations need to mirror that.

Who does the HR function serve? There are many stakeholders and vested interests, and HR can succeed only if all these are constantly tended, like spinning plates. The answer to my question is clear – HR serves the business. Building a healthy business is good for every stakeholder. This health – in terms of financial, ethical and human success, so that people can perform at their best

– is as complex as any conundrum on the planet. No other function is held accountable for so many aspects of it. No other function has to manage such complexity, or has such broad reach, and that's what makes HR so exciting.

Valuing conflict

If HR doesn't successfully anticipate and manage conflict, it ends up getting caught out. As individual professionals and leaders, and as a function, it's easy for HR to get stuck, as one HR director called it, as 'piggy in the middle'. A classic conflict is lived out daily in how performance issues are managed. HR will explain employment law and values, and a production manager may still say, "They've got to go, they've had enough chances, I've got my targets." The manager finds HR's advice inconvenient, is unwilling to follow the procedures to the letter, and escalates the issue to a senior business leader, who says to HR, "Yes, I know we have to follow procedures, but this person still has to go."

The business leader has a choice in that moment – back HR or back their manager. At least, that's the way they see it. Upsetting HR will probably have less impact on their performance bonus than upsetting their team member. For most HR people, the greatest challenges for their professional and personal integrity will be presented by senior leaders. Standing up for what's right is a political minefield, and we'll explore that when we look at another enabler, **Push** (Chapter 8).

Most of the time, HR knows when it is heading for conflict. Many of HR's decisions and actions do reflect the needs of a range of stakeholders, and they need to be seen to do so. It helps when HR explains the full rationale, even when the staff feel they've said it many times before. It's acceptable to take an employment law risk if the commercial risk is, on balance, greater. It's HR's professional responsibility to make sure that business leaders are clear about the risk and why HR recommends a particular course of action. Then, the ownership of the decision and its consequences lies within the business.

In one role, in an IT company early in my career, I was recruited to set up a UK HR function. I had to create policies from scratch and, partly because I was so under-resourced, I recruited a group of managers who seemed to 'get' good HR to help me. We started with the usual core policies that I had from previous companies, which were legally sound, and went from there. We discussed whether and why they were needed, and then worked on the wording. I can't claim that I fully anticipated it at the time, but this paid dividends in two main ways.

First, the policies did reflect the actual life of the organisation, the challenges we faced and the culture we wanted to build; they were written in the right language. Second, the managers who had been involved would really fight for them. They weren't known so much as HR policies; more as those of the policy group.

Sharing ownership

Most HR functions don't have this opportunity; much is already well established, and that particular organisation was small enough for me to be able to say, for example, to a sales director, "Talk to Mark [a sales manager who was on the policy group]; he'll explain why we put the policy together this way." This illustrates a central point – policies that tend to be given to HR to 'police' should be more proactively owned by the whole organisation.

We could call managers' lack of ownership an enormous 'cop-out', and HR people reading this will have seen that play out many times. We could go back to our patient and doctor analogy. The patient needs some kind of treatment, because something isn't going well. As in the case of eating too many doughnuts, this may because the leader or manager has failed to control their natural impulse, for example, to micromanage, or fail to manage. The manager likes eating doughnuts, resents someone telling them that they need to stop eating them, and will probably try to blame the doughnuts.

Who owns the doughnut policy? The reason this analogy works is that HR is not in the room when the manager is actually eating the doughnut. Leaders and managers need to own their own behaviour. But what drives their behaviour? This is what HR needs to understand in order to spin those plates and achieve balance.

HR's decisions need to incorporate the inputs of all stakeholders and be seen to do so. The interests of varied stakeholders can be explicitly built into policies: state why something is important and why it must be upheld. The role of the HR professional helps enormously in the translation of policies, so that they can be made meaningful for the client group.

Maintaining balance can be particularly hard for the HR business partner, in fact, as there can be a tendency to 'go native'. The HR business partner role can be a fulcrum for these tensions between stakeholders in a way that challenges as well as frustrates. A good HR business partner will build very strong relationships within their client groups, and often experience a dilemma between upholding the interests of their client leaders and those of HR. In fact, this is a good indication that the HR business partner is genuinely striving for balance.

Trust and transparency

Trust in HR helps the organisation to value its policies. If someone is asked, "Do you trust HR?" they are likely to evaluate the HR person they have the most contact with. Indeed, we have found in some organisations that a person will say, "I don't trust HR, but I trust my HR business partner," or vice versa.

The integrity of the HR function is vital, as is the integrity of the people within it. Leaders, managers and staff need to feel they can trust HR. I have, actually, just stated an opinion as if it were a fact. Consider your own view. Is trust vital to the performance of the HR function?

My own view comes from working at all levels in HR, as well as working as a consultant with HR. There are times when the organisation needs to learn the truth, and HR is the most appropriate conduit for that. Truth and trust are closely related. HR is also often held accountable for the actions required when hard truths emerge.

For example, if someone is being bullied, whatever their race, sexuality, gender, appearance, or for whatever reason, the organisation must investigate and take corrective action. We have learned that severe damage can be caused to reputation, brand and sales from tolerating behaviours that are inappropriate and, frankly, wrong. There are many degrees of this, from outrageous harassment through to subtle innuendo. We always knew it was wrong, and these days we know the business rationale too. News can spread to the outside world in a way that can have a serious impact on a company's ability to operate.

In today's world, most agree that action needs to be taken when wrong is committed, and we celebrate when perpetrators are exposed and punished. High-profile cases in the media reflect the less public but equally important cases that are managed every day by HR.

"You should tell HR," an employee will say to a colleague suffering inappropriate treatment or bad management. Most organisations would want this to happen, and in a supportive environment. What would stop them talking to HR? Confidentiality, perhaps – can they trust HR to keep it to themselves if they're not ready for it to be managed? HR people tread the confidentiality tightrope every day. It's a constant balancing act between the interests of the employee and those of their manager; HR has to respect both.

I was caught out once, by a director – let's call him Martin – who told me he'd been contacted by a headhunter and was talking to him about a role. I didn't feel torn about that and kept Martin's confidence. However, when I found out that the headhunter was the one we were using ourselves for a senior recruitment, I told my boss that I thought the headhunter was using his knowledge about our company to target people – which is definitely not ethical. I didn't say it was Martin, and my boss spoke to the headhunter. It turned out that Martin hadn't been headhunted, but had approached the headhunter. If Martin hadn't boasted that he'd been approached, there would not have been the ethical issue for me to manage. Martin had been naïve, but the outcome was a rather hurtful conversation for me when he said that he could no longer trust me.

As I reflect on that situation, which was, thankfully, the only time anyone told me that they felt they couldn't trust me, I realise that my trust issue was actually with the chief executive. He liked to handle the headhunters himself, which is not unusual, because bringing them in for a nice piece of work is a great way to position yourself for your next career move. But it was he who told Martin that he knew he was looking around. HR often needs to have a kind of 'triangulation' in place with trust. When the chief executive worked out it was Martin who was planning to leave, he should have been conscious of the need to protect my trust with Martin.

Trust is a minefield for HR, and it has to make some tough calls. I'm sure I'm not the only HR leader who has had to sit opposite someone talking about some their plans when, in fact, I knew they were going to be made redundant very soon. That feels deceitful, but it goes with the territory and HR learns to live with it.

Trust and transparency came quickly to the fore during 2020, when people were asked to work from home. Many had wanted to work from home before that and had been turned down. It seemed too difficult to be able to supervise people's work – to make sure they were doing what they should be doing. That was turned on its head overnight, and most people proved that they could be trusted.

Is your default position that you do trust people, or that you don't? This is a question for each of us as individuals, for HR functions, and for business leaders. The other question, which is entirely tied in with this, is how to measure people's productivity. If we think back to my section in Chapter 1, From loom to Zoom, we can see how technology has largely freed us up from the need to be supervised physically. There are still some situations where this is helpful, for example, training staff in call centres, but many where there is absolutely no need to be able to see the person physically.

Balancing trust and measuring productivity

So, how do we measure productivity? There is a lot of discussion about outcomes-based performance measurement, and I'm sure this will evolve very quickly and well. This may align with changes in designing people's work so that it aligns more to projects than to roles. Technology is a major factor in redesigning work and measuring productivity. We can see when people are working and when they're not. "I could see that their green light hadn't been on for three hours," an HR director said to me about a team member who'd been working from home. So, out of sight isn't out of mind. Technology gives us the means to find out what people are doing.

There is an ethical question here: just because we can, does it mean we should? The chief executive of a processing company I worked with was an IT whizz. He had designed the company's core IT programs himself. It was also known by some that he had retained in that system a way of seeing what everyone was doing; he had a kind of back door into the system, which he checked regularly. Employees had worked it out; he would say things that he could have known only by going into the system that way.

He was demonstrating an absolute lack of trust, and it undermined the culture fundamentally. It also undermined his own performance: he would pick up on detail and miss the big picture. The impact on the team was stultifying. They'd play it safe, wait for him to tell them what to do, and then he'd complain that people didn't use their initiative.

It wasn't that people didn't think he had the right to know what was happening, it was that he would check what they said. Did they have a guilty conscience about something? I couldn't be sure, but what was clear was that he'd built a window into the system that was one-way, and he wasn't honest about it. Transparency wasn't in place, and it was seen as unfair and suspicious.

Transparency is a vital tool for HR and can be built across the organisation to support positive values. We will explore further how to get more clarity and shared understanding into the open between HR and business leaders.

HR as a curator of organisational values

Trust is likely to be a vital element in a broader set of values that HR works with every day. When I've worked with organisations to develop a new set of values, we've started by researching what it is that the different stakeholders value. Typically, there are three main groups that we end up focusing on: customers or community, employees and business. Happily, their main interests largely overlap; everyone wants a business that's financially sound and can invest, employees who do good work and enjoy it, and happy customers who want more.

It's how you get there that then starts to distinguish one organisation's values from another. I mentioned earlier the differences in culture between an organisation that relishes innovation because it needs to grasp market opportunities quickly, and an organisation that must have safety in mind at every step because it operates in a potentially dangerous environment. Both organisations need both innovation and caution, but they need to decide which messages are most vital to their success, in the current context, and make those messages louder than others.

We could say that values statements are a kind of volume control: they tell us what we need to be talking about, because we can't focus on everything all of the time. Some years ago, a financial services company came up with values that spelt 'HOT' – honesty, openness and truth. This was a particular response to a period of dubious integrity in that company. There could be no doubt where they wanted their people's focus to be.

Values are tested in a disciplinary or performance situation every day. If someone has tried their best, and failed, they have done their best to live the values. The reasons for their failure may relate to their ability to do the job, and this requires a different approach. HR continually has to make the distinction between attitude or intention and capability, and take the actions that the organisation has agreed it should take.

HR carries serious and important responsibility. It helps if the organisation's values fit with your own, because then you can carry the responsibility more lightly. Much is about managing risk. The risks are to humans, and to governance, as well as commercial. In many decisions, all tend to be combined.

The risk that's normally most visible for HR, because they will be in front of them, is the human. The impact on the person will be at the front of the HR professional's mind as they watch to see their responses, and gauge their honesty, commitment and intention. Whether you're a business leader or an HR leader, you will not be able to ignore the person. However, caring for the human doesn't tend to build HR people's reputation as credible influencers.

Here lies a central challenge for HR, and why this enabler called balance is so important. The human element is only one of the plates that HR needs to spin, and the organisation's values should help it build the whole ecosystem in which people can be successful.

Consider the values espoused by your own organisation. To what extent do you think about them and use them in your everyday working life? How relevant are they to the challenges that you face in reality?

Values should give clear messages about what's important, and especially about frontline delivery to the customer. For example, HR often faces a dilemma between 'correctness' and commercial realities, and can earn the reputation of putting obstacles in line managers' way. Typically, line managers will push for quick action while HR knows the risks of not following due legal process. HR has to balance both when making decisions about how to advise the line manager. As we discussed in Chapter 5, looking at **Connection**, where trust has already been established, and the HR manager or business partner has invested in helping the line manager understand the full implications of their actions, this will be a much easier conversation.

Upholding values is key within organisations. Values provide the language to describe the spirit in which an organisation wants its people to work. They explain what you want from people, behaviourally, right across the organisation. HR has the best view across the organisation, and unique reach into every corner. It is vital for HR to maintain this overview, and to work with senior leaders to build and maintain the desired culture. HR holds this together on behalf of the whole organisation, and needs to remain impartial. While other functions may push for their own agenda, HR must be seen as honest brokers.

This is why it is so vital for HR staff to live the values themselves as well as upholding them across the organisation. Business leaders must also be actively involved in this; they can delegate the responsibility for ensuring that the values are upheld, but need to be held accountable for leading and being role models for the values at all times.

Balancing the short term and the long term

I promised to come back to this gritty yet fundamental dilemma for HR. Actually, this challenge is shared by every function and organisation. As mentioned earlier, a quick fix operationally often has longer-term implications for values. Almost everything in HR requires a good thinking through rather than a simple solution — unfortunately.

One typical challenge is in deciding who to promote, and how. I had just joined a company as head of HR when the chief executive decided to promote an engineer into a new managerial role that he'd just decided to create. To him, this was straightforward: the team needed more direction, and he knew who he thought was the most capable. This snap decision led to discontent in the team and made it more difficult for the new manager to succeed. That chief executive was not cognisant of the implications of his decision on values, and how this would be seen as unfair. Talking this through with him was a difficult conversation.

Demonstrating integrity in decisions about people's careers does take time and demands rigorous process. A great example is that of development centres, where those who are unsuccessful also benefit from good quality feedback and development, so that the process is enriching for everyone. It does take significant investment, however, and takes up the time of various stakeholders.

Important decisions need not only to be fair, but also to be seen to be fair.

HR needs to educate, explain and make transparent the tensions that exist within choices, and the potential benefits of choosing the higher-quality solution instead of the quick fix. You don't win the right to do this straight off. It takes time to build a relationship where you can shift the conversation towards the longer-term implications.

An HR director told me that she knew that she was getting somewhere with her HR business partners when a business leader said to her, "I look forward to my HR business partner meetings because we get to talk about the future." The point here is that the line manager was talking about the future of *his* team and *his* operation. That's what success looks like in business partnering – you're so focused on the other person's world that you can navigate to the future and build it together.

It had taken some time to get to that point. HR has to invest time to build its understanding. This is achieved conversation by conversation, as trust is built and more information, insight and ideas can be shared within a space that's mutually supportive. Then, HR can explain how it sees the various interests, and together they can work out a solution that balances these.

Coaching plays a key role here too. As mentioned earlier, HR can use questions to enable a colleague to look differently at a situation and explore options. Coaching is a short-term versus long-term dilemma in itself. HR people often ask themselves, "Shall I go into coaching mode here, or just give the answer?" As is the case for any leader, the real question is often, "Do I have time – or should I make time – to do some coaching here?"

More often than not, the most expedient thing to do is to give the person the solution. For knowledge workers, such as engineers in particular, that's their comfort zone: fixing the problem. Explaining the long-term implications of that choice – whether to fix it or coach it – is another excellent illustration of creating clarity about the impact of leaders' actions. For example, a consistent theme raised by participants on leadership programmes is that of work-life balance: specifically, working long hours.

For leaders, coaching their team members so that they can take on more from them is a solution that's time-expensive in the short term, but frees up time in the longer term. They soon realise that it benefits the team and builds a team culture of trust and growth.

Most people don't realise, consciously, the impact of the choices they make every day. In your own role, think of a recent occasion when someone came to you with a problem. How did you respond? Did you offer a solution, or use some questions to help the person to think it through for themselves? If you did make this choice consciously, what helped you to decide? Were you thinking of your own need, for example, to deal with them quickly, or theirs, say, to develop? Whichever you chose, what did it cost you? There is always a cost, even when we choose the option that looks the most expedient.

Building the long-term health of an organisation is core to the purpose of HR. Organisations can't grow if the people who work there don't grow. Getting the most from every employee makes financial sense. Markets and customers engage with people who are engaged. There are so many stakeholders involved in organisational success, and all of them matter. HR has the task, and the privilege, of balancing all these.

Here are some questions for you to consider:

- Look back at the stakeholder map that you created earlier. Which of those stakeholders have needs that conflict?

- When have you felt yourself in a situation where you had to balance a person's trust with your ethical responsibility to your organisation?

- With which stakeholder have you achieved the greatest transparency, and how did you achieve that?

- When have you felt your personal values challenged in your role?

- What are your most challenging conflicts between short-term results and longer-term implications?

CHAPTER 8

Push ⬆

HR faces complex challenges – it's about more than the numbers, it's about hearts and minds, and behaviours. HR needs to push forwards, and at times also push back – to stand up and speak out.

Dave Ulrich called this, "HR with attitude". It's a useful quote because Ulrich implicitly respects the value of HR, and also urges more courage and ambition. HR comes historically from a place of administration, ensuring correctness and managing risk. Now that we have achieved the shared understanding that human performance drives business performance, HR has the opportunity to grasp, or to consolidate, a position of true leadership.

The central challenge for us in this chapter on push is that transformational HR happens conversation by conversation. An elegant and intellectually astute strategy creates a comprehensive and cohesive overarching framework for change. It paints a compelling picture of the future organisation so that people can understand purpose and direction.

However, strategies are ultimately realised through behavioural change. If you do what you always did, you get what you always got – whatever the strategy paper says. Changing what people actually do, or how they do it, demands careful planning and persistence. Within the strategic vision, what will people be doing, saying or even thinking differently?

In this chapter, we will look at how to create this shift within the HR function itself.

Transformational HR

I mentioned this earlier, and now will look more closely at what it means. In this section, I will explore this in relation to strategic interventions and in terms of conversations between the HR leader or professional, and the line leader or manager.

Put simply, by *transactional* we mean a programme, project or conversation that leads to a short-term impact or quick fix. This is often appropriate – we can't be transformational all the time. However, there are very many occasions when we can grasp the opportunity to do more, to push things forward more proactively. Today's organisations demand that we do.

By *transformational* we mean an activity or conversation that adds more lasting value and provokes fresh thinking or a change in behaviour. This is the challenge we urge you to embrace within this chapter on push.

Here are some illustrations of the distinction between the two, and you will see how these can apply to projects as well as to individual conversations or interactions during meetings:

Transactional HR	Transformational HR
Clarity on short-term objectives	Establishes the long-term vision
Perpetuates control structures	Creates a climate of trust
Solves problems personally	Supports others in solving problems
Maintains or improves the status quo	Challenges and changes the staus quo
Plans, organises and controls	Coaches and develops individuals and teams
Guards and defends prevailing culture	Challenges and creates an evolving culture
Power from their position	Power from influencing others
Authority from the organisation	Authority from trust and respect

Transformation is indeed definitely more likely to be achieved by strategic projects that encompass the whole organisation, and that are well led and resourced. Much research has been done on how to achieve this – how to design a programme that will pull the right levers, get the desired result. From the top, it looks like an elegant cascade that maps out the required steps. That doesn't mean, however, that it wins support from everyone, everywhere, all the time. That's why I've brought this in again to this chapter about push.

Many organisations have created transformational shifts in culture, for example, from autocratic to developmental, which have resulted in higher engagement and productivity, retention of key people, and innovation. These decisions were likely to have been driven more by data than by altruism. Thankfully, there is now much data that supports more humane and enjoyable leadership and management styles – it leads to better business results.

There is a natural tension between intellectual analysis and operational reality – we could say it's between 'top-down' and 'bottom-up'. Looking from the top, leaders do need to be able to pull threads together into one cohesive picture that has clear strategic imperatives. To do that, they have to aggregate data, clarify themes and patterns, and relate them to their markets as well as to the views of analysts about their sector and its future.

From the 'bottom-up' view, that is, for the people who are interacting with customers every day, or in production facilities, their world is naturally smaller, their perspective narrower. This is as it should be because we want their focus to be clear and uncomplicated. However, this means that some intelligent translation is essential to ensure that a strategic initiative makes sense to all. We could say that it should be turned into something that looks like a simple menu, which creates an appetite as well as ensuring easy digestion. Without this, strategic initiatives can make it look as though leaders live on another planet.

This kind of strategic project inevitably falls within the already complex remit of HR, which finds itself in a kind of 'selling' role for the initiative. It really helps if the HR people believe in it themselves. HR's own beliefs about any initiative, policy or process are naturally critical to its ability to promote it, and I will come back to this in another section in this chapter.

A particular person's perspective depends on where in HR their role sits; they may have shared in the top-down creation of the project, or be part of its operational implementation.

In a recent consultancy project, aiming to do a great design piece on a development programme for HR business partners, we looked into the issues being faced by our participants. One of the issues, ironically, was the number of programmes being rolled out by the centres of expertise, that is, within HR. The HR business partners were finding the volume difficult to cope with, and this was also increasing the level of resistance they were getting from their client groups. It wasn't good for their credibility with business leaders and line managers either: their responses would typically be, "Not more stuff from HR." The HR business partners clearly felt 'done to' rather than involved and eager clients of the intervention, however valuable it may have been.

HR can find itself caught in the middle of many situations, one of which may be caused within its own function. The centres of expertise need to understand the pressures the HR business partners face at the front line as well as the reality of business. The HR business partner needs to support their colleagues who are trying to bring in best practice, which will lead to success in the long term. The quality of dialogue and collaboration *within* the HR function is, therefore, also critical.

When everyone works together in HR, and pushes back both ways, they share their insight – top-down and bottom-up – and the results can be dramatic. If we add to this the opportunity to act as facilitators and engage leaders and managers at every level and throughout the organisation, all this positive energy is unstoppable.

One critical question is: how do we ensure that we reap the full rewards of a strategic intervention? Consider your own organisation. Think of a recent intervention; it could be any function: HR, or finance, IT or marketing.

- What were the strategic aims, and how clear were you about them in your own role?

- How well understood were these aims across the organisation?

- How was it received?

- What actually happened? What do people say about it, unofficially?

- What benefits has it delivered?

Think about what helped in areas where success was achieved, and what happened where it wasn't; these will help you in your next project.

When we think of the changing world of work, HR has a critical role to play in achieving some real transformation. In Chapter 1, I talked about how the opportunities to embrace AI fully may require a complete re-engineering of roles or, indeed, a move entirely away from the concept of the role.

How could this really work – making technology add far more value to everyone's work? I wanted to get my head around this and did some research for an article on our website. It was surprisingly difficult to find examples of organisations that had really cracked this. Even within knowledge management, where I'd expected there to be plenty of knowledge transfer, for example, from specialist engineers, into a system, there were few case studies of success. There is no shortage, however, of suppliers wanting to make the technology work.

My conclusion was that embracing AI is far more bottom-up than people think. It's less about IT than I'd thought, and more about enabling people to work out what they can 'delegate' to their computer. The most vivid example was that of an intelligent whiteboard in a meeting room. People use their amazing human intelligence to open areas to explore; the whiteboard 'listens' and intelligently offers data of many kinds to inform their debate.

This is a fascinating subject, and I could go on, but my point here is to illustrate the exciting role that HR can play in this. In fact, only HR has the reach for this. But HR has to push its way into this, or it will be run by others.

The threat is always there of the most exciting aspects of work being taken away from HR. Many aspects of HR have already been outsourced. So far, it has tended to be the more routine – transactional – areas, or the specialist areas where consultancy organisations can provide the required expertise.

Every organisation needs a function that will be both the oil and the glue – to promote smooth running and hold everything together. HR has a track record for achieving this. Moving to the next level of leading transformational change is challenging. Some HR functions are known for this, and some are not.

What are the reasons for this? One reason must be the level of maturity in the relationship between the chief executive and chief HR officer. They need to be fully aligned and mutually supportive. To achieve this, HR must be represented on the board and involved in all strategic planning and decision-making. Another reason can be the reputation that HR has across the organisation, as discussed earlier.

Without having good relationships in place, HR can be neither the oil nor the glue. It is the quality of the interaction between HR and business leaders and managers at all levels that drives high performance in people – from the board to the front line.

HR must continually push itself forward. It is well placed to avoid a disconnection between elevated strategic discussions and operational reality, across the organisation. Achieving real change demands taking a leap. HR has hard data, experience and insight, and living connections into every corner, which can help to ensure that the leap will be the right one and that there will be a safe and successful landing.

Achieving transformation that sticks

This is a continual, multi-level campaign that is won conversation by conversation. Let's imagine that you have in place, from the top to the bottom of your organisation, trusting relationships between business leaders and managers and your HR people. They talk frequently, can bring up whatever they like, share information easily, and explore what's coming in the future as well as what's happening right now.

Getting your key messages across can be as effective and as automatic as the way the plumbing in your house works. You probably don't think about your plumbing much, unless it goes wrong. Most of the time, you take for granted that when you turn the tap water comes out, and you can turn it off just as easily.

Good relationships are like a reliable, constant system that's ready to circulate your message. The HR function can be your most effective communication system. Your HR people have the full picture, can adapt the messages to suit their audience, and find the right moment to drop them in. They use the moment to relate organisational values to individual situations.

Let's take the classic situation where a line manager comes to HR with a performance issue, and the example of a value, let's say 'learning'. They don't say, "Here's the policy, look at page 5." They listen, find out how the issue developed, and help the line manager to learn, as well as solving the immediate problem. They will be explaining how to live the value (without mentioning it, probably) as well as how to be a role model for it.

HR is a vital and ever-ready channel through which organisations can communicate, in many subtle ways as well as directly, with leaders and managers at every level. HR does not achieve results itself; it achieves through others. This is a central challenge for HR, as it makes it so difficult to provide hard evidence for its ROI. However, using HR as a channel for communication is a central opportunity for every organisation that is often underused.

When we think about winning over hearts and minds to an intervention, or to core values, or a project, it's important to be clear about who really *owns* it. As I mentioned earlier, this can be rather opaque. For example, a sales training initiative may be driven by HR or by L&D, but it's owned by sales.

This can provide a situation where we need to establish clarity and push back. In my European HR role, we rolled out some sales training designed in the US. Because it was training, it fell to me in my HR role to implement it – ironically, to 'sell' it to the sales directors in each country. Looking back, that's just not right, but I didn't think about that then and I'm sure this happens to HR people all the time. We were part of a global organisation where the head office was a little distant. So, the regional directors in charge of sales asked me to get it moving – that got their tick in their box.

What I learned when I went out to see each sales director was just how different their ways of working were in each country, and how the skill levels of their salespeople differed. This sales training involved a clever questioning structure and worked well in the US, but in Italy, for example, there were more basic skills that were more urgent. Teaching them to run before they could walk would be a complete waste of time and money.

First, I had to get my mind clear about what I thought was right. I'll come back to this, the personal dilemma, in the next section of this chapter.

My point in this section is that HR doesn't have transformational conversations by pushing a solution that just isn't right. HR's credibility is at stake, and its ability to influence in the future.

We talked earlier in the chapters on **Perspective** (Chapter 6) and **Connection** (Chapter 5) about being politically intelligent. Having a proactive strategy for this situation is by far the best solution. In this instance, if I had had stronger relationships further up in the sales organisation, I could have acquired and deployed more of their influence. Having said that, there were various causes for this situation: global HR and sales lacked understanding of the real capabilities of salespeople in different markets, and indeed of the markets themselves; European HR and sales weren't positioned to influence the training before it was selected; and the culture existed that you didn't argue with 'corporate'.

So, there I was, expected to make it work and feeling stuck between a rock and a hard place. I know I'm not alone in this. A former UK chief executive of a global US company said to me recently, "You'd know it was wrong, but you just couldn't turn it off."

Enabling HR to build trusting relationships with leaders and managers, and ensuring that this happens, creates the channel through which HR can win hearts and minds. When it's the message, or the intervention, that you want to get right, HR can share its insight and help it to land well and work.

For its part, HR needs to be strong in making its case – whether for or against – and push for what's right. Whether it's a strategic intervention, or iterative change, the reality is that you achieve change one person at a time. Each person has their own decision to make about whether to get on board or not, and those individual decisions build into commitment that has real potential for lasting change.

Leading self

We can't lead others unless we're clear ourselves – about what we stand for. Whether we are a chief executive or a chief HR officer, a line manager or an HR business partner, we can demonstrate far more compelling leadership when we know ourselves.

What happens if our organisational values and personal conscience aren't aligned? We are weakened. It's uncomfortable, it affects our intellect, and it undermines our ability to build trust. The concept of psychological safety is much better understood today. We've always known intuitively that we perform better when we're relaxed and with people we trust, and now we have the science to prove it.

How do you decide when you want to stand up for something, or express your concerns about it? Undoubtedly there's a political element to this if it could be a 'career-limiting' moment. Some dilemmas may be fundamental, and you will need to build a strategy to work through them. Sometimes we decide to come to terms with something because there are larger issues at stake. However, many dilemmas come up in the moment and we have to decide in the moment whether to push forward or push back.

Knowing what we stand for, personally as well as professionally, helps us to make the right decision in that moment, and be convincing. Making choices consciously is one of the areas I find leaders can access most effectively, immediately they're made more deeply aware that there is a choice.

Let's take work-life balance, which is always a major topic when you work with leaders, "I'm worried I'm letting my daughter down; I don't spend enough time with her," one said to me once. In another group, there were no fewer than three leaders going through divorces who felt that their work had taken over their lives, with traumatic consequences. Did they consciously choose to work late repeatedly, take calls at the weekend, continually check their phones for messages? I'm sure they didn't. The point here is that they didn't consciously choose at all.

How clear were they in their minds that their families were their priority? All the leaders I mention were full of regret that they had allowed their commitment to work to overshadow their commitment to their families. In fact, they had lost sight of their commitment to themselves and their own happiness. Work can be addictive.

In organisations, we all face difficult dilemmas. We have to be careful about what we choose, and when we choose it. The best way to prepare ourselves to be strong is to create our own platform of clarity to stand on.

Let's go back to my sales training dilemma. Forcing the local sales team to undergo the sales training wouldn't just have been a waste of time and money, it would have undermined their confidence in their sales management, and in me. Imagining the salespeople going through this kind of training, imagining how confused they may feel by it, and even stressed, was hard too. Training should be a positive and motivational experience as well as developmental.

Despite pressure from my own boss, the HR vice-president in the US, I just wasn't prepared to do it. HR should not be associated with something that has no value in it.

In stating my rationale above, I am revealing my own beliefs and values, about myself and about HR. What are yours?

What did I decide to do? We used the same sales trainer but got him to give the salespeople what they actually needed, which was much more basic. I didn't tell the exact truth when I reported upwards, but my conscience was clear because I'd done what I thought was right. The tick was placed in the box, and my credibility and integrity remained intact. What's more, sales in Italy increased steadily.

We need to be clear about our own, personal, beliefs. When we are not acting in line with our beliefs, it is hard to find leadership in ourselves. This does not mean to say that you can always be in situations where you're fully aligned with your organisation, or your boss, or your targets – this will always be a struggle. I know from working with thousands of leaders over the years that this kind of contentment rarely exists. In fact, at that level, it might be risky if it did.

However, we can be clear about what the dilemmas are, bring them into our intelligent mind and think them through, as I suggest in Chapter 6, about **Perspective**. When I look back on my corporate career, one of the many things I would do differently is to spend much more time looking, objectively and analytically, at what was happening around me and why.

Only then can we be clear and develop our approach to dealing with what's facing us. We may say to ourselves, "OK, I can live with x, but I can't live with y." For example, I've heard leaders say that they can live with the target they don't agree with, because they understand intellectually how targets get cascaded down – but they're still very frustrated about the situation it puts them in.

When I then ask the question, "What is most difficult for you, personally, about that?" I get information that reveals much more about what's important to them; several leaders on the same programme will give different answers, which can each lead to a different solution.

For example, one may say, "What gets me is that my boss clearly doesn't respect me." Another will say, "How am I going to motivate my team when I don't believe myself that we can do it?" Yet another will say, "I work so many hours already, I'm worried about the impact on my family." There is then a sequence of questions that can be used to help them to illuminate their situation. Other leaders listening to this learn as much as the person under the (gentle) spotlight. These questions include:

- What is the main challenge that you would like to overcome in your leadership?

- What is that costing you?

- What are your practices, that is, the things you actually do, which lead to that?

- In that moment – what are you choosing?

The aim is to make many of the thought processes, of which they are not fully aware, much more conscious. Beliefs work at a fundamental level within our psyche and are so natural within us that we can be unclear about them, until we hear ourselves saying things such as, "People should…" That's a dead giveaway.

Intelligent people can change their behaviour easily when they change what drives it. You will have been on an influencing skills workshop, I am sure. I am also sure that you don't put it into practice all the time – no one does. Influencing itself is not difficult – intellectually we know how to do it. Actually doing it involves starting at a deeper level.

Deep clarity about who we are, what we believe in and what matters to us is vital to our fulfilment as human beings. It is also a powerful tool in fulfilling our potential in our role, and our function. Clarity helps us to be courageous and strong, because we know what is at stake and that we are right to push forward for it or push back against it. We could even consider it a weapon. Let's call it our light sabre.

Positively challenging

Once we're clear, and our mindset is in place, many issues immediately seem lighter. Removing the burden of confusion helps the brain work better and explore solutions with more energy and creativity. I talked much earlier in this book about how we 'leak'. Then, I was talking about some negative 'leaking' of frustration. Now, with clarity of thinking and the confidence that this gives us, we 'leak', or even radiate, credibility.

If you don't *believe* it, you cannot *be* it. If you don't believe that HR should be front and centre of the organisation, it won't be. Let's look for a moment at that tricky word 'should'. It's immediately telling us that this isn't actually happening. It's a 'conditional' tense, that is, suggesting that in some future circumstance this may happen. It leaks lack of belief.

As a function, HR can decide to just *be* it. Don't ask for permission. Just know who you are, the value you add, and develop your skill and confidence to *be* the way you want to be. You'll need to work out when (as explained in Chapter 5, about **Connection**) to *respond to*, *predict* and *create* opportunities to *be* it. If you're all doing, and being, the same across the function, your organisation will sit up and notice.

Being positively challenged is valued by intelligent leaders. They see the opportunity to look at something differently; spot a different way forward; identify a factor underlying an issue that they had overlooked. I talked earlier about using powerful questions, and this is the most effective and supportive way to challenge. It's also diplomatic, which makes it highly politically intelligent. Our aim isn't to look cleverer than the other person: it is to help them to access their own resources.

Again, in that last sentence, I've revealed my own belief about the value we add, and it's my mindset as a coach. I do not believe that I know the answer, or that it's my job to work out the answer. It's extremely helpful for me, as an executive coach, not to know much about the coachee's job or situation. I can ask naïve questions from a place of professional equality.

What is your own view about being challenged? I'm guessing that will depend on how it has been done. Consider an occasion when you've been challenged recently – whether at home or at work. Think of one that was constructive, and one that was not, and reflect on why. It's likely to be a combination of the message, that is, the content of what was said and whether or not you liked that, and how it was transmitted, that is, the behaviours used by the person and the intent that you sensed underpinned them.

Enabling HR to positively challenge leaders and managers is core to its ability to promote the people agenda at every level. Strategically this is self-evident. Operationally this needs to happen, and I'm sure does happen, within a myriad of conversations every single day in every single organisation. Good HR people are good at this.

Research tells us that this is highly valued by chief executives and business leaders, and that there is scope for more of this, and at higher levels. This is how HR leaders build their credibility and influence.

Resilience and emotional intelligence

Standing up for something, pushing forward and pushing back can be stressful. However, stress doesn't arise from the situation we are in. It develops from our reactions to it: how we interpret it, filter it into our store of other similar situations and allow it to colour how we see the world, and ourselves within it. I'm no psychologist (as any psychologist reading this will be able to tell), but age and experience have helped me to learn much more about how the human brain works, and I love reading about neuroscience. I urge you to discover more about this (see Resources) and hope that, like me, you will see that your intelligent mammalian brain can truly help you to manage the responses from the more primitive parts of your brain.

Our brain can take us by surprise, as I learned when coaching an HR director at a university. She had been in the role for around six months and was preparing to present her HR strategy to the board. I knew she was well regarded, and her strategy was sound, but I could see she was feeling blocked. She also had a strong track record in previous roles, and I asked whether she had had a similar experience to draw on, which is often a great way to enable people to access some positive resources. However, she started to cry. It emerged that in her previous role she had been humiliated by board colleagues in a similar setting.

The learning for both of us was that she had had no idea that this was so close to the surface. Intellectually, she knew that that experience wasn't her fault and that in fact in that role she had experienced something close to bullying. Intellectually, this one bad experience should be far outweighed by her previous, excellent relationships with boards. However, her intellectual brain was not in control in that moment.

Many of you will have read Daniel Goleman's work on emotional intelligence (see Resources), and he offers a useful framework for managing our emotional responses. He recommends that, first, we recognise the emotion and listen to it. After all, our body is trying to tell us something. Only when we pause to understand our emotional response can we decide, rationally, what to do about it.

All emotions are valid. Neuroscience now challenges many previous beliefs about emotions, for example, the view that they are separate from our thinking processes, and in a different part of the brain. It's all much more of a mush than that, in terms of our brain structure and the way our intellect and emotions work together. Emotions are, it seems, a much stronger input to our so-called 'rational' thinking than we previously thought. One way of looking at it is that the human brain is not rational, it is *rationalising*. We thought we knew when we were 'post-rationalising', after the event, but actually it's happening in the moment. Our brains use every input possible to help us work things out, and not all of them are factual data.

The physical responses we have are important messages too: the increased heart rate, the flushed feeling or headache. They aren't very articulate, because they were evolved many millions of years ago when we had much more limited choices. The stark choice between fight or flight does seem rather primitive, but in fact we're still binary. We decide whether to approach, or to avoid. 'Decide' may be a rather sophisticated word for the mix of physical, emotional and chemical reactions that happen without much reference to the frontal cortex.

When you're in your next meeting, consider which of these two options you're leaning towards − possibly even physically. Are you feeling comfortable, and coming closer as in approaching positively, or is something not quite right so that you are moving back as if to avoid? Tapping into this response gives you more information that you can check out with your brain and use to make intelligent choices about what to do next. You can draw on your resources of well-honed behaviours and skills, and rise above your initial, potentially irrational, response.

I talked earlier about the importance of deep clarity, and that helps in our emotional resilience too. When we think of heroic endeavours − perhaps Luke Skywalker with his light sabre, or Nelson Mandela with his use of words − we see that their belief, their commitment, was absolute. In fact, let's use a quote from Mandela's favourite poem, *Invictus* by Henley, "I am the master of my fate, I am the captain of my soul." (see Resources).

Being true to ourselves is something that we can do for ourselves, wherever our life or our work takes us. The good news is that it helps your business to succeed too.

Here are some questions for you to consider:

- In your organisation, to what extent is HR known for pushing forward and pushing back?

- What kind of support do you typically experience in your organisation for change initiatives? Why do you think this is?

- What do you stand for in your role? How would people know that?

- What would you like to feel able to challenge? What would help you?

- If you knew you could not fail, what great thing would you dream of doing?

CHAPTER 9

Rigour

HR can't pass 'go' without the credibility that comes from reliable, accurate and up-to-date operational and advisory services – delivering what you promise day in, day out, getting it right and making it better.

Rigour is about keeping a tight ship, whether it's a cruise liner or a dinghy. Whatever your HR strategy, this is about delivering it to a high standard and within budget. HR is delivered through many very different processes, from payroll to talent management. All these processes require inputs and engagement from other parts of the organisation, which can be difficult to manage and to measure.

There is a lot of risk involved in HR, especially when you don't have direct control over those who are implementing your policies. Often, HR people are the ones who have to sort out the consequences when their own policies aren't followed. 'Policing' gets HR a bad name and doesn't sit well with being seen as partners. So, again, it comes back to the quality of relationships and the level of respect and credibility that HR commands.

In 2018, an employer lost an employment tribunal in the UK because the line manager said, "I did what HR told me to do." This was seen as a landmark case because it meant that HR is held accountable for educating, influencing and winning over hearts and minds of line managers, rather than just telling them what to do. Making sure that a legally correct procedure is followed isn't enough; there needs to be evidence that the employer has got their line managers fully on board with what's right and fair.

How can we be sure that HR is taking the right action, at the right time and in the right way? There are some instances that are clear, transparent and measurable. There are others that are blurred, clouded by multiple levels of delegation, and scattered into every corner of the organisation. To what extent should HR be held accountable for the behaviour of every leader and manager?

There is no simple answer to that question, but we will explore it in this chapter, as well as looking at how HR measures can be developed.

Measuring HR's performance

There are different ways of looking at this. One is to look at hard measures, such as employee retention. Losing people you wanted to keep is very costly in terms of recruitment costs as well as hassle, onboarding and lack of continuity. In the case of employee retention there are benchmark figures for each sector: in retail, say, 40% or more may be deemed acceptable, while 20% in engineering may be seen as high.

However, what we're doing here is measuring something after it's gone wrong. It is a valid and valuable number, because it draws attention to issues that must be managed. It adds more value to measure the factors that lead to this consequence, because this shows where you can invest to get a better outcome.

The recent trend of continuous listening in organisations has been an inspired development from engagement surveys, because it measures what is happening at key points during the employment lifecycle. There is now a strong mix of annual strategic surveys and tactical 'pulse' surveys, combined with attractive apps that make the interaction with these surveys much more engaging.

We also have sophisticated offerings in people analytics, which support a real drive towards much more 'data-driven' decisions in HR. Data is powerful, and HR leaders are learning how to leverage this. There are many eager suppliers in this area if you'd like to find out more.

HR must demonstrate that it is focusing in the right areas. In Chapter 10, which deals with **Focus**, we will explore how HR *decides* on its priorities. In this chapter about rigour, we concentrate on the actual *delivery* of that, and on how that delivery is measured. The data now available gives us a better understanding of both, but still gives only part of the story.

I've used the term return on investment (ROI) in this book. What does that really mean in HR? So much of what HR does is noticed only when it goes wrong. In fact, it can be said that success in HR can mean doing yourself out of a job. If everything goes as it should, the HR manager's phone never rings with a performance issue or a grievance.

One client used the analogy of toilet paper. Why is the corner of the toilet paper turned up when you go into your hotel room's bathroom? It's quite simply so that you know the housekeeping staff have serviced your room. I was working with a group of high-potential field engineers who repaired X-ray machines in hospitals. They had become so good at fixing machines virtually – doing preventive maintenance remotely so that they didn't go wrong – that, when it came to renewing contracts, customers would say, "But we haven't seen your engineer." The participants were given this challenge to work on as a project, and the analogy worked brilliantly for them.

This analogy raises a similar question for HR. Let's say a director says at a board meeting, "The company next door has saved 30% of its HR budget by outsourcing. We should do that too." What would be the response from the board at your organisation? Consider this for a moment. Perhaps part of your HR function has already been outsourced, and for purely transactional services this can be a welcome solution for all concerned.

The point is, if they need to have a discussion about it, HR's case is already lost. You'd hope that the director wouldn't even have considered it in the first place. I would suggest that, ironically, the board's decision won't be based on hard data at all. Board members won't decide because of employee turnover or engagement as a number; they will decide based on the credibility and influence that their HR function has to do something about that number.

Senior leaders do not criticise HR's technical knowledge and expertise, such as in employment law, recruitment, talent or development. Indeed, throughout this book we take that as a given. It is how those capabilities are deployed that make the difference. That is what we researched, and we worked out how to measure it.

HR must gather convincing evidence of its impact, and this means supporting hard data with stories and illustrations. We talked much earlier about the strategic narrative and the HR narrative that should flow within that. This provides the proper framework for the data and stories.

The story, therefore, needs to start with the organisation's unique business model. Imagine it as a machine that has various switches and levers. When we drive our car, for example, we know that when we push the accelerator pedal, we get more fuel to the engine and this results in more speed. Every organisation has its own accelerators, brakes, steering devices, suspension, comms technology and so on.

When I'm working with clients, I like to get my head around how their organisation works, and often use the success model tool that I mentioned in the chapter about **Perspective** (Chapter 6), with an example https://www.enable-hr.com/success-model which draws a distinction between enablers and outputs: it shows how one activity drives another.

To recap, the success model enables a clear focus on what drives success – it starts with what is it that you want customers to do. There is great value in getting on to one piece of paper how your organisation (or your part of your organisation) works. This enables HR to clarify how its activities help to drive that organisational machine in particular.

This can then be built into an HR Success Model, which clarifies the linkages between HR's activities and their impact. These linkages are often self-evident to HR but can be made more explicit to business leaders to help build a sound business case for investment in resources or interventions. For more information about this, see https://www.enable-hr.com/HR-success-model

HR's narrative must include a cost-benefit analysis, as expected of any function. In this chapter about rigour, it is important to highlight how important it is to use this story, with all its high-quality data, to prove the value of the results achieved: the ROI. Bear in mind constantly the questions – how are we going to prove that this was a) the right thing to do, and b) we have achieved it effectively?

Reliable, accurate, appropriate – no excuses

If HR doesn't get the basics right, it won't be taken seriously in other ways. Running efficient services is vital to the organisation. As I mentioned earlier, when HR services are being delivered without a hitch, no one notices. When something goes wrong, say an error in your pay, you're likely not only to notice, but also to tell others.

This kind of operational excellence runs alongside various projects, some of which can be complex, for example, strategic changes to the structure of reward or roles. The implementation of these projects demands the same high levels of thoughtful accuracy and thorough completion. This isn't just about efficient processes: there is a human reaction at the end of the trail, which can never be overlooked. A new structure, process or intervention may look great from the altitude of the boardroom but can fall short of fulfilling its potential because it is communicated poorly.

Governance falls into this area of no compromise. HR people are risk managers as well as developers of human potential. That one sentence combines two totally different perspectives, and yet HR needs to balance both. Let's take diversity and inclusion (D&I) as an example. Sound and fair D&I policies are now, thankfully, recognised as true drivers of high performance and HR has worked tirelessly to promote the spirit of inclusion as well as the law. This is also a dangerous area for reputational risk and demands careful monitoring and managing through others.

Reporting with integrity is another absolute requirement of HR. There are legal reporting requirements as well as ethical. HR's challenge is always to provide senior leadership with information, not just data.

This is a short section, because it is clear. HR must deliver what it promises. I will explore later in this chapter the challenge of negotiating those expectations so that they can be met.

HR as expert adviser

Giving high-quality advice is one part of this challenge, and the other is being listened to. In so many cases, there is no power as such, only influence and credibility. Let's take a performance issue. HR advises the line manager but has no control over what actually happens in the conversation between them and their team member.

Helping the organisation to operate within the law is a serious responsibility and HR will be held accountable for it. At the same time, any HR person giving advice that doesn't appear to take into account the business realities will be seen as inflexible and unhelpful. Therefore, the challenge is behavioural as well as intellectual – it's not what you say, it's the way that you say it. The questions you ask help you to get to the right solution, and to win commitment to it.

Every conversation about individual issues – for example, performance, absence or any other of the typical ongoing challenges that line managers face – builds into a bigger picture. These conversations are pieces within a much larger jigsaw of culture, and alignment with values.

At more senior levels, HR people must reflect the issues that their stakeholders are talking, reading and worrying about, to show that they're up to date with the strategic context.

The responsibility, and opportunity, for HR at every level, is to widen the conversation and move it forward. In my business partnering matrix below, I clarify two directions in which HR can move the conversation. All four modes are valid, and built on trusting relationships:

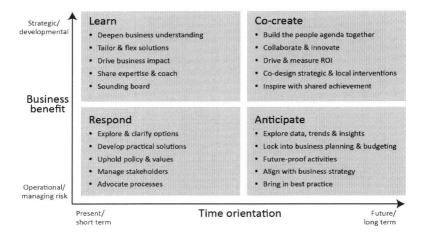

The vertical axis encourages HR to embrace business realities and acquire depth of understanding of the business. The horizontal axis is about orienting the conversation to the future.

The purpose of introducing it here, in this chapter about Rigour, is that HR must always be fully aware and sensitive to the bigger picture. These two dimensions will help HR to ensure:

a. that it is making the organisation future-proof; and

b. that it gets the best value from its HR budget by ensuring that its solutions are fit for purpose.

Therefore, every conversation with a line manager or leader provides an opportunity to ramp up HR's impact. One critical outcome of these conversations, for example, about performance issues, can be to minimise disputes – risk management is important. However, every thread within the conversation can be followed up into a conversation that's more developmental for the line manager. This is how HR builds management strength, day in, day out. It moves from the transactional to the transformational.

HR's specialist expertise is shared with line managers in a critical interface that is a testing ground for advice and judgment. There are some situations where a formulaic response is what's required, but others that require everyone to take a step back. At some point, HR can identify patterns or themes that demand a less situational and more strategic approach. It needs to judge when it is wise to take a deeper look, to explore root causes and engage with other stakeholders.

There is so much that can be learned at this interface between HR and business. As I have said before, good HR people quite rightly regard themselves as businesspeople who happen to be in HR.

However, our aim is to get the best from HR expertise and insight, and from those outside HR, which is why I am using this distinction again here. The quality of that critical interface can drive so much learning and improvement.

HR will be held accountable for its ability to move those conversations forward as well as delivering flawless services. In return, with its enhanced credibility, its advice is more likely to be valued, respected and put into action with good grace.

Continuous challenge

This spirit of enabling the organisation to move forward also applies to every HR process. Tightening up operationally is a constant pressure, while also challenging the very nature of HR activities that may no longer add value.

Let's take the example of performance management processes. In the period around 2017–19 there was some eagerness to dump the performance appraisal meeting and, sometimes, even the link between performance and pay. The debate raged around changed management structures, more flexible roles, the time it takes to have a good meeting and the fact that the decisions around performance ratings had fallen into disrepute.

Much of the criticism was valid, and the dissatisfaction real. However, organisations need a framework for evaluating and rewarding performance if they are going to encourage the behaviour they want. The fault wasn't in the principle; it was in the implementation. This particular debate has now largely gone full circle; organisations are returning to a structured approach to performance management but doing it much better.

I mentioned earlier the company that decided to do some development with leaders and managers to refresh performance management and remind managers how to use the ratings.

Running these workshops demonstrated to me that these conversations haven't changed for years, since I was in an HR role myself. Leaders and managers give a multitude of reasons why they want to give someone a higher rating, not all of which are related to their performance. "They'll leave if they don't get a good pay rise," or, "They're ready for promotion but we can't offer them anything yet," or even, "We know the company down the road is paying more."

Who owns performance management? Few people would disagree that developing the performance of an individual is the responsibility of their line manager. In today's matrix structures, there may not be one clear line manager, but there is generally someone appointed as a performance manager who must ensure that they support the individual. Therefore, the responsibility for developing individual people lies within the line.

However, the philosophy and principles tend to be within the remit of HR, and these must be protected, primarily in the interests of fairness. The spreadsheets come through to HR with the proposed performance ratings, and HR's role is to calibrate them across the organisation.

Let's go back to my own situation with two managers who had contrasting beliefs about whether a high rating or a low rating motivated improved performance. Faced with two spreadsheets, one smattered with A ratings and the other with D ratings, when I knew the relative performance of these two teams was similar, I had to pick up the phone and talk it through. This is such a tricky area for HR, and the pay decision is where it all comes to a head. The standard distribution curve is unpopular but it's difficult to see an alternative. Let's say you have a budget of 2% of salary to award to your team. It's the finance function that is responsible for this budget, with the functional head. HR's role is to support the fair distribution of this budget, but it's HR that gets the flack for the decisions, with a manager even blaming HR for a drop in the rating that they shouldn't have revealed in the first place before it was agreed.

This kind of tussle can become very frustrating for HR people at all levels. HR and line managers can fall into the trap of parent and child attitudes that drive behaviours which then perpetuate the cycle. This is why the real accountabilities need to be made clear, and demonstrated by role models, from the top. The annual reward cycle is a prime opportunity for leaders across the business to proactively support HR – when it is in the room and when it is not.

Good HR is continually evolving. Various demographic trends are coinciding with the need for flexible and virtual working. It will take some time for these changes to be fully tested, improved and bedded in. One change (for example, flexible hours) has many implications and has to be thought through – what it means in terms of what you want to reward and develop, who you want to recruit, and how to continue engaging with and retaining your key people.

Technological changes can offer huge efficiencies as well as engaging ways to communicate with employees. HR technology is a growing field, operationally and in the provision of data. We'll come back to that in Chapter 10, which looks at **Focus**.

It's the way all these activities need to be integrated – leadership, data, competencies, reward, development, and so on – that presents HR with such exciting and complex challenges. Values and business priorities need to be threaded through everything, consistently and coherently. This is the most powerful way to build real clarity for every employee about what's important – and that's what drives the performance you want.

HR has to keep working at this from every angle, from rigorous governance and operational efficiency through to ensuring that the values are lived, behaviourally. Strong systems are key to this, but the real driving force is the quality of the relationships through which everything is played out.

Here are some questions for you to consider:

- Regarding people, which risks most concern you in your part of the organisation?

- In your experience of what HR does in your organisation, what would you most like to improve?

- How self-sufficient are the leaders or managers in your area regarding HR? (for example, to what extent do they demonstrate confidence in making HR-related decisions?)

- In your own relationship with your organisation, what causes you to feel less committed?

- In which area in HR would you like to see more rigorous measures?

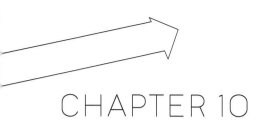

CHAPTER 10

Focus

Taking the insight that's been gathered, and using that to make sure that HR's efforts and resources are invested in the right areas – in order to get the best value for the business.

There are always great demands placed on **HR**. There is work that absolutely must be done: predictable activities such as governance and essential services, as well as the unpredictable issues and challenges that can walk through the door of any **HR** professional at any moment. No other function has to deal so frequently with such a range of situations – disciplinary matters, health issues, bereavement, grievances and more – where you can't say, "I'm busy now, how about next week?" because it has to be dealt with right now.

Dealing with problems can cause a downward spiral into **HR** becoming a reactive function. This can be a self-perpetuating syndrome; if you can make the time to coach line managers, then fewer issues arise, and you have time to add more value. If you hardly have time to draw breath between urgent issues and have to find the quickest solution, you end up making the decision yourself, going into telling mode and nothing changes. Client groups go into compliance mode, which leads to lack of accountability, and blame.

I know from my clients and my HR network that pushing against this continues to be a major challenge for HR functions at every level. While those in specialist functions, such as talent or reward, may be one step removed from the urgency of many issues, their active support and understanding can play a huge role in driving the credibility of the function as a whole.

The distance, or separation, between the different parts of the HR function, is a factor which itself needs to be managed. Indeed, some specialist functions such as L&D may not regard themselves as part of HR at all. However, pulling all the threads together of all aspects of employee performance will enable organisations to drive the best returns from HR. When programmes are fully integrated, mutually supportive and cohesive, they deliver more.

Some tough decisions have to be made about what can and will be done, and what can't. How should HR decide where to focus its time, energy and effort? In a function that can be pulled in many different directions, how does it involve others in those decisions, and manage their expectations?

Any professional function must undertake careful planning and budgeting to ensure that it operates within set constraints. Regrettably, time isn't elastic, nor are budgets. There are many robust discussions across organisations about expenditure, and HR must be as rigorous as any other in planning intelligently what it will commit to do and what it cannot do, and renegotiating if necessary.

In tune with reality

The closer HR keeps to what's really happening in the organisation, the better it can demonstrate its deep understanding. These two positive forces continue to drive a virtuous circle: better understanding enables better solutions, which enable better communication, and so on. The relationship between HR and line leaders and managers continues to strengthen and, with it, HR's credibility.

This reminds me of my analogy of the plug and the socket, and the power of the current that can flow through when channels are clear. Focus, too, depends upon the viability of that current, and understanding that resistance also has to be anticipated and managed.

Let's imagine that HR has developed a brilliant intervention, let's say, developing leaders to retain key talent. A generous budget of £1m is allocated – it's a large company. There are consultants to pay, development workshops for L&D to design and run, and communications programmes.

The dates are scheduled and joining instructions are sent out. The fulcrum of all that investment, all that preparation, is the training workshop where managers will learn how to manage their talent more successfully, for example, to do more coaching and trust-building.

However, something has been overlooked. The reality for the managers booked into those workshops is less predictable, less controllable than the process of designing it. Let's take Simon, who is a production manager. His goals are all centred around productivity, and his monthly targets are non-negotiable because other teams depend on the items he produces – or they won't meet their targets either. They have a full order book, thankfully, and demanding customers. Simon's really worried about taking two days out for this workshop because he's one team leader short and has some new operatives.

On the day of the workshop, a second team leader calls in sick; he's been showing signs of stress for some time and the doctor has signed him off. Simon calls his boss for advice, and is told not to worry about 'the HR workshop'; they can't risk not meeting their targets.

The irony is evident. The stress and pressure are likely to have been caused by poor management of talent and, in the critical moment of truth, Simon's boss chooses the short-term priority over the long-term solution.

How does this play out in your organisation? Consider a situation where you have experienced a similar dilemma, either for yourself, or regarding a planned intervention that didn't get support in that last critical decision of whether to get the attendance.

Thankfully, there is another episode in this story. Simon tells his HR business partner, Kim, that he can't make it. He wants to, but he can't see how to get there. Kim understands the strategic importance of the talent programme, and also the operational pressure. She knows that Simon's boss does too, but that in the moment couldn't think of an alternative. Kim calls him and helps him work out that he could move another production manager, who has a more stable team, across for those two days. Simon made it into the workshop.

Kim successfully managed the resistance. It is very possible to have strategic support for an intervention where even the leaders don't appreciate the actual difficulties involved in getting people at the front line fully engaged. Senior leaders do not always put sufficient effort into communicating their commitment to HR or L&D programmes through their own leadership. Some believe that their leadership responsibility ends once they've signed off the budget.

Let's go back to our £1m. If just 10% of the places in that workshop are left empty, £100k has been wasted. That does not include the loss of the value of the learning.

Getting the right focus

HR scores real points when it proves that it understands reality. Many aspects of reality, such as the levels of attrition of talent, can be measured. However, those measures are retrospective, and HR must demonstrate that it understands the underlying causes and how they relate to those outcomes – and help others to understand.

To do that, HR needs to be in the loop, and up to date. It needs to understand its audience and their market, that is, the managers through whom it delivers its results. Demonstrating pace and agility, and giving practical help to managers when they need it, builds HR's credibility hugely. By responding with an eager attitude, demonstrating positivity and applying their expertise in a practical way, HR people display skills and behaviours that are highly valued.

How can HR get the whole picture joined up? I talked in an earlier chapter about the top-down and bottom-up challenge, and our talent management programme is a good example of this. On the front line, pressures tend to be more immediate and short term. However, it is at the front line that any organisation's real value is generated – customers served, products created, sales achieved.

How can HR get frontline managers to take a longer-term view, and senior leaders to support them in getting strategic programmes welcomed and embraced at the front line? In this section we're focusing on reality, so let's start with the operational kind of conversation.

Working with HR business partners gives valuable insights into how these conversations work in practice. As a result, I developed the business partnering matrix that I mentioned earlier on page 146. This works in fact for any central function:

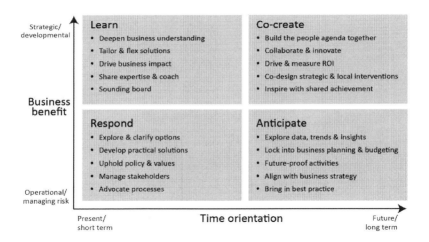

This offers two questions to ask yourself when you are in any conversation:

a. To what extent are we talking about the realities of our business (not about HR)?

b. To what extent are we talking about the future (not the present)?

One important point to reinforce here is that all four modes are valid, depending on what you want the outcome of your conversation to be. All four modes are also built on trusting relationships.

The value of making this point in this section is that you do not earn the right to talk about the future until you've earned your stripes by talking credibly about the present. HR must demonstrate its real insight into operational reality – as well as its genuine interest in it and how it works.

In terms of our four boxes, it most often works best to start at the bottom left. "What's happening for you right now?" "What are you working on?" "How can I help you with that?" In practice, that's more comfortable for us, as humans; we're getting our bearings before we step out.

HR has the real advantage of a multi-level structure – professionals working at every level, building relationships that provide windows into the organisation – and channels for that current that can deliver power to every corner. Getting the most from that structure, and collaborating within the function, is an additional challenge and opportunity for HR.

Getting the right focus for HR's activities depends on operational understanding as well as effective relationships. They lead to rigorous debate and working together to build the best solution.

The reach is there within the organisation to ensure that interventions are designed so that they really do deliver the required return. We will come back to this shortly. When any part of the HR function becomes too distant from reality to ensure credibility at the front line, it does so at its peril.

Bringing best practice

This is where it does pay to start with the big picture. Evidence-based decision-making is valuable in HR as in any function and, in this area, much of the most useful evidence is generic. Examples include demographic trends that affect every organisation; performance and productivity figures; engagement statistics; and research papers that paint the picture of the future and the challenges it will present.

Many organisations will be able to compare this with internal or specific contextual data; people analytics; engagement surveys; and sector and market trends. In addition, as the other functions do, HR will have insights from the latest thinking in their profession. Then, of course, we have consultants and suppliers offering clever solutions that bring latest technology, and experience from other organisations.

There are many areas where we really don't need to reinvent the wheel. Many of us bring into any new role our experiences from previous organisations – indeed, this is likely to have been part of the decision to recruit us. However, challenge is key to focus.

How do we decide how far to push innovation, while keeping our feet on the ground? How do we balance high intellect with practical realism? Several times, I have been brought into organisations where one of the large strategic consultancies had prescribed a solution that didn't work in practice. In those instances, it was often because the later stages of implementation had failed, rather than because the strategy wasn't right. The effort required to build the leadership and management of it that had been underestimated – the changes in behaviour and the commitment that would make the change stick.

The elegance of a solution can sometimes be its downfall. Less is usually more. Solutions must be designed for inclusivity – of intellect as well as all other factors of diversity. People have to be able to *get it* without too many layers of reasoning, not because they're less intellectually able, but because they don't think like strategists. That's just as well, because they're dealing with practical realities every day in their work, and they're busy. They need to be able to relate the strategic intent to their own work.

Ideally, there will be an appetite for an intervention before it reaches people. We know now just how important it is to engage people's own sense of their worth and their autonomy; this can be undermined when change is forced. We demonstrate respect for people when we show that we understand their reality.

The best way to create an appetite is to be clear about the benefits, to position what you're doing within a context that makes sense to your audience, and keep working at it until you hit gold.

One heart-warming example of this for me is the work I did with the field engineers I mentioned in Chapter 9, about **Rigour** – you may remember the toilet paper example. I want to explain how we got to something as strategically valuable as the project about making sure customers really valued their contract when it came up for renewal.

A quick recap. This programme was designed because these engineers had very little visibility in the organisation; it was difficult to spot potential because they spent most of their time in their cars and at the locations or regional offices across Europe, the Middle East and Africa (EMEA). This lack of visibility was two-way: the engineers couldn't see their career opportunities either. So, this was an international programme to get the engineers into a situation where they could be seen and they could shine, and to spark their ambition.

We built into the programme many factors that would lead to them looking great at the end of the two modules, including research tools and presentation skills. They had the chance to present to very senior leaders the outcomes of their projects. To start with, the projects were selected in a rather arbitrary fashion; HR would ask the leaders for topics that the engineers could work on in a meaningful way, and they would be important but not often implemented because they weren't part of anyone's goals. We certainly did achieve the outcome of seeing the cream rise to the surface: several of our participants were promoted, and this programme built the reputation of being pivotal in identifying talent.

However, it was frustrating when some of their projects came to nothing. The ideas and solutions were strong, but they weren't fully aligned. One simple change made all the difference: the timing of the question. Instead of HR asking, "What projects can you suggest for our participants?" after business goals had been set, they repositioned and re-timed their request thus, "When you're having your strategy meeting, identify some areas where the insight and ideas of our field engineers, and their real knowledge of our customers, would be useful to you." This was welcomed, the appetite created for the participants' presentations went to a new level, and the leaders' real engagement in debating their projects was rewarding for everyone. Several projects were implemented, and a real buzz was created.

Achieving the full potential of any intervention is an iterative process. You cannot have all the information, and deep understanding, at the start. Provided you are open, curious and courageous, you learn as you go along and can continue to push for even more complete integration into the business. The quality of your relationships, as always, enables the trust and openness that support this kind of continued dialogue.

It's too easy just to move on to the next thing before you've secured full implementation of the last. I recall a statistic that 80% of the benefit of a project comes from the last 20% of implementation, and I totally believe it. Sadly, it's often the most tedious part where for you it's become repetitive, seems less fun, and you'd rather go on to the next thing.

However, that feeling may in fact signify that you've reached a point where you can learn even more. It's become more comfortable. Perhaps it's time to tackle another angle, one that seems harder and maybe you thought you could avoid – a difficult person, perhaps, who still refuses to get on board. Working that through can lead to even more credibility and extend HR's reach even further.

Making it work, and making it stick, is how we achieve the full value of our £1m. A lot of translation is required to get something from strategic intent to full operational value. Sometimes HR has to translate ideas into leaders' language, and sometimes translate leaders' language into something more digestible to their client groups.

Making something work on the ground requires cooperation, and sometimes collaboration too, in order to get the best value from everyone's intellect, perspective and intent. HR people play a pivotal role as facilitators and problem-solvers on the ground as well as being ambassadors of the strategy and the spirit behind the intervention.

Driving focus from the top

It is vital for HR to tune into how business leaders think. We have been exploring the challenges involved in winning active support, and whether this is for a particular investment or for good HR practice, it has to start at the top.

I talked earlier about the importance of the ability of the chief executive and the chief HR officer to understand each other's goals and perspectives fully. If the quality of the dialogue – honest, curious, challenging, robust – is not in place at the top, then it's much harder to get this working at other levels. Both the chief executive and the chief HR officer need to be role models for a productive relationship, and to align their teams. Even in today's more flexible and matrixed organisations, there is a line of command and authority, especially financial. When it's a question of getting value for money, this must be used.

At the most senior level, it's mainly about numbers. It has to work this way, or it would be impossible to pull all the data together in a way that helps decisions to be made. HR doesn't tend to have a great reputation for playing the numbers game; I hope it is different in your organisation.

Business language has to come first; HR language must come second. This is why we developed the HR Success Model, which we mentioned earlier and welcome you to explore https:/ www.enable-hr.com/HR-success-model

The starting point for every organisation is to be clear about the results it must deliver. Only then can anyone, in any function, explain why they do what they do.

I experienced this first-hand in a memorable lesson on influencing from Alice, my global HR vice-president boss in my pharma role.

Our global president, Joe, was visiting Europe, which was a big deal. Alice invited me to the meeting and asked me to watch what she did.

One subject that Joe found confusing was that of the huge differences between sales achieved per sales rep in the 23 different European countries we supported, and also between their expenses. There were many reasons for this, including the way different health and regulatory structures worked, as well as cultural factors. However, rather than going into any of this, Alice said, "If we could show you a way to understand that, Joe, would you give us the budget for it?" Joe said, "Yeah, sure," and that was it. We positioned our competency framework as a way of comparing the relative performance of sales reps across Europe.

Joe didn't want detail, and he didn't want to hear the word 'competency'. It's HR jargon. What he wanted was to increase the level of sales that each rep could bring in. He'd looked at the spreadsheet of numbers that showed an absolute number and he wanted that number to move up. He'd calculated quickly that if all reps achieved sales similar to the best, that would mean a huge increase in sales.

Ours was a sales-driven European regional office. The products were produced in a separate division, which had completely different metrics. This made it easier to focus. In our part of the organisation, every number would be related to sales. This can be dangerous, as it can lead to short-termism which, as I've mentioned, is a tension that works against HR on the whole.

What numbers can help you or your HR team to focus on the same priorities as senior leaders?

Building clear and measurable linkages between behaviours and financial outcomes lies at the heart of this challenge for HR. Thankfully, today's organisations place far more emphasis on the behavioural qualities of the chief executives they recruit than they did in the past. In addition, many reward systems have been redesigned so that behaviours are rewarded to the same extent as results. In principle, if someone doesn't behave well, they can't get their pay award even if they've outperformed in terms of their financial targets. Enacting this will be one of the critical moments when senior leaders need to stand up and stay true to the values they espouse.

Simplicity is also vital. Organisations are so complex. In the telecoms company I mentioned earlier, there was one number that everyone talked about. Any investment would have to be related to its impact on that number.

Courage is also crucial when working at that level. It's easy to back off from raising a concern about something that doesn't feel right when a) the people involved have real seniority, and b) you expect them to be smart enough that your instinct will be proved wrong. If we don't get the access we need to the people we need to talk to, it will be very hard to deliver good results. It should always ring alarm bells when people make it difficult for us to dig.

I learned this the hard way. I was asked to work with two teams who weren't getting on, in a tech company. One team included the tech gurus, and the other was customer-facing. They'd recently been restructured into these two teams. One team missed the customer contact while the other team was criticised for the quality of its technical specifications to the gurus – so people kept crossing boundaries.

The respective leaders of these two teams were extremely difficult to tie down for my preparatory calls, and then kept them brief, blaming time pressure. The other participants I interviewed were much more vocal, but still didn't mention the core issue. The workshop began well, with sticky notes all over the wall clarifying the key processes and the pain points between the two teams. However, it gradually emerged that there was a fundamental conflict between the two leaders, and it was this that was leading to all the issues.

This intervention was the wrong solution because of an incorrect diagnosis and, as such, was a waste of time and money. HR was acting in good faith when it brought me in, as both leaders had requested it. The whole project had seemed rather rushed from the start, and this was a warning sign too. If you haven't got time to make sure that an intervention is going to be a wise investment, apply the brakes. There is more to lose than the cost: there's your credibility, and that's precious.

Senior leaders have little time for conversations that don't get to the point. Explain your own thinking and explore theirs. Alongside this direct style, demonstrate business acumen using astute numbers that you understand fully and can illustrate. HR must be clear about how it sees the real value, or deliverable, and get this across with conviction. Bringing credible behaviours with astute intellect creates a powerful package.

Manage expectations

The strategic clarity that we develop then helps HR to decide what it can do, and what it can't. Another question is about what HR will do and what it won't. What I mean by this is that it isn't only a question of resources, it's also one of accountability.

If we take the concept and spirit of business partnering (never mind the job title), this conveys the building of a relationship that brings two people together: two brains, two ways of seeing the world, two contexts, two sets of expertise. By exploring each other's worlds further, step by step, they learn together how to leverage both. They are building an open and trusting relationship within which they can develop powerful solutions that are fit for purpose because they are based in reality.

Creating partnership is, therefore, a journey towards achieving focus. There is a lot of explaining for HR to do along this journey, to clarify the benefits of working in a different way. Let's take the example of an HR director, Sarah, who wanted to drive the full potential of the role with her team of HR business partners. One element was to train and educate the business partners, as you would expect, in the full implications of shifting away from adviser to partner.

Another vital element was to manage the expectations of their internal clients. This meant explaining clearly to them, "If we continue to do this, we can't do that." She explained that if we continue to manage issues for you, this takes up all our time and we can't work with you to anticipate issues and manage trends, which will make your life easier in the long run.

The HR business partners took opportunities to explain the choices when they arose, "I could take this issue off you, and that's how we've worked before. However, if you manage this kind of thing yourself – with my support – we can free up more of my time. With that time, I could help you with x or y, and you've said that's something that would really help you." This eventually led to the line manager saying, "I now look forward to my HR business partner meetings because I get to think about the future."

Often, HR people have several client groups and need time to take a view across them. In the challenge I mentioned earlier, about having to earn your seat at the table, I took my roadshow around Europe and set out my stall. "This is what I can do for you," I said.

There were several surprises in terms of what the country managers wanted me to do. One was the need for a career structure for their head offices. These were relatively small teams, with skilled professionals who got to know the business and customers and it was a real blow when they left to develop their careers. This hadn't been on the radar of the regional directors.

It proved to be an extremely productive project, and cost-effective because it benefited several client groups. The financial benefits were demonstrable in terms of retention and less business disruption.

The technique I used was simply to explain, and to enquire. Once they understood more fully what HR could offer, I was able to explore with them the issues they were facing and develop ideas. It sounds obvious, I know, but somehow we can lose sight of the obvious in our busy jobs. We end up being driven by our to-do lists, meeting agendas and inboxes, and hearing the loudest voice rather than the quiet need.

The project went into my HR strategy and budget, and also into the three-slide explainer that became the introduction to most of my presentations, "This is where we add value and why, and this is what we're going to deliver this year." This, too, helps you to manage expectations – by showing what you *are* doing, you are giving a balanced and constructive view of why you can't do everything.

HR should continually challenge what it does and be brave enough to ditch things that no longer add sufficient value – such as old processes or gathering data that's no longer useful – and explain why, "We're doing this because… and we've stopped doing this because…"

James Cracknell quotes the challenge that his Olympic rowing team used constantly, "Will it make the boat go faster?"

Planning and project management are key skills for HR, to work out how far the resources will stretch. Contracting with client groups is an opportunity for HR to get in control of this, and we have more on contracting on our website https://www.enable-hr.com/contracting-for-HR

While some HR functions like to work with a formal service level agreement, for many their commitments are a more movable feast, and contracting can be a constant negotiation.

There is a gravitational pull towards short-term fixes and operational pressure. The most dangerous situation is one where you risk disappointing stakeholders. The most lasting impact is likely to be achieved from activities that have a future focus, and yet the pain points for stakeholders are often urgent. The only way to manage expectations is to keep talking about the choices with which you are confronted, and to share the accountability for decisions with business leaders and managers.

The purpose of focus is to ensure that you invest resources in the right place and get the credit for being at the heart of business success.

Here are some questions for you to consider:

- How do leaders in your organisation see the priorities for HR? How do you know?

- Where can you bring more best practice or latest thinking into what HR does?

- How do you feel about the choices HR makes about where it focuses?

- Where are the most challenging pinch points for HR in your organisation, that is, where do resources not keep up with demand?

- What do you think HR could do less of?

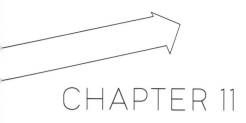

CHAPTER 11

Empowering HR to step up

This is the central invitation in this book. Whether you are a leader of the whole organisation or of the HR function, you will want to inspire your HR people to make even more impact.

In this final chapter, we bring together all the strands from earlier chapters into an overarching strategy for building HR's credibility, influence and confidence.

Because every organisation is unique, there is no one recipe for great HR. I offer you here some final questions so that you can build your own roadmap and decide what you want to work on. I start here with the strategic overview, but you may choose to start with one critical stakeholder in one business area. The most important decision is to start.

Our seven HR Enablers (see page 44) support you in answering all these questions. There is more information on https://www.enable-hr.com with additional resources.

What is the purpose of HR in your organisation?

In Chapter 2 we talked about the strategic narrative, and the importance of building real purpose into that statement to make it compelling, and then translating it so that it is meaningful to the next level. I suggested these examples as illustrations, but of course yours would be relevant to your context, sector and culture:

> Organisation:
> "Our technology improves lives around the world."
>
> Strategic HR:
> "We create the conditions for expertise to thrive."
>
> Operational HR:
> "We build bridges towards great people outcomes."

How powerful would it be to make this top-level, strategic discussion about HR's strategic narrative an actual collaboration between HR and business leaders? This is an excellent place to start.

In my experience, there is insufficient discussion at top level about what HR can contribute, what it looks like when it's working well, and who owns it. This lack of clarity and ownership cascades, implicitly, down the levels. It's reflected in how people talk about HR, as well as in how proactively they engage with HR. No one says out loud, "Let's disrespect HR," but it may be part of the culture and it's too easy to get away with it in some organisations because of HR's legacy.

Having a strong sense of purpose gives you power. HR's activities do have real purpose in the world. HR matters. Every single person in employment is impacted by HR policies, processes and, most importantly, people. From the moment they notice a job advertisement to the day they leave, employees rely on HR. However, as I mentioned earlier, HR can be almost invisible when this is going well.

Going unnoticed can be a sign of success, but not of political intelligence. At the highest level, HR leaders must turn over the corner of the toilet paper. We were here, we did the work while you weren't looking, and we left you to get on with your day.

A clearly articulated purpose statement for HR is a powerful leadership tool, for HR people and for winning support from leaders for HR's work.

What do you want people to say about HR?

Do you want people to say, "HR is caring," or, "HR is tough?" I'm guessing that you wouldn't pick either of these words for your HR brand. So, what would you choose? How do you want people to describe how your HR function is *being* in the organisation?

Many aspire to be seen as a trusted partner. How could you develop a strategy to be seen in this way? These four key elements of trust are relevant here too when you are working out how to be seen as you want to be seen. Decide, together, how you want to come across, and:

- Be *consistent* across all your activities and teams, whether strategic, specialist or operational. Live your brand across all your policies, projects and behaviours. Get your whole team to repeat the same messages.

- Be *reliable* and deliver what you promise, whatever situation you are in. Manage expectations so that people know where they stand.

- Demonstrate your *competence*; do great work and make sure stakeholders understand, and value, the rationale for your actions or recommendations.

- Show your *commitment* to your business and your stakeholders. Leave them in no doubt that their interests are at the top of your agenda.

When are the moments when we can *be* how we want to be seen?

To recap, there are opportunities that you can *create, predict* and *respond to* – the moments where you create an impression. As we explored earlier, this needs to be a planned and conscious process.

Look at your diary in a new way – spot the opportunities that already exist, and plan how to make the most of those. You may have casually disregarded them in the past, but those are the building blocks of your reputation and too important to throw away.

Create new moments, where you are making the move and setting the agenda. It may be a relationship you want to improve; for example, "The way you and I work together is very important to me, and I'd like to book an hour of your time to talk about how we can move that forward."

Or, you may want to create an opportunity to move to the top right of the business partnering modes matrix (page 158), for example, "I want to find out more about what's really important in your part of the business. Then we can work out some future plans together that will really add value to your team."

Create strategic moments. Pinpoint opportunities for you to get across your strategic intent. Prepare your core messages and get them into every important meeting and conversation.

Be yourself. Authentic leadership is compelling, and it doesn't matter what level you're working at. Everyone in HR is a leader. If you're feeling conflicted, frustrated or not fully aligned, address it.

What is the vision for people in your organisation?

This is the powerful coaching question that I mentioned earlier. If everything went well, what would it look like? What would people be doing, saying, feeling, celebrating? That strategic vision must be built together with leaders from every function.

The leadership of that vision should also be shared by every leader and manager. It is the vision of how they want their people to be treated and included as well as how they should be led and managed. It just happens to be the remit of HR to design it, support it and, where necessary, enforce it.

Then, it can be translated into relevant priorities and workstreams. There is much that goes on year after year in HR, and it is vital to continually challenge established work routines to check whether they still add value. Taking full advantage of technological advances is a wonderful opportunity for HR, which many are already taking.

At every level, HR must have a seat at the table and use it well.

Is HR part of the top team?

Here we must mention the question of whether or not HR is represented on the board. The numbers are improving, but there is still a way to go. Larger organisations are more likely to have an HR director who is a full board member, while smaller companies may place HR within the remit of the finance director.

It is almost impossible for the people agenda to be effectively created, promoted and achieved without top-level representation. It also gives a weak message about the importance that the organisation gives to people matters.

If you're not in the room, you can't contribute.

Build the people agenda together at the highest levels, and then create a multi-level partnership that makes it happen. The HR leader has a vital role to play, not only for their function but also as a trusted partner, sounding board and coach to the leadership team.

To what extent do your HR measures reflect what you really believe is important?

When HR's purpose is clear, it is far easier to determine the measures that will be most informative. The day-to-day work is vital and must be celebrated, for example, low recruitment costs and low or no employment disputes that take up endless time. These run alongside measures that more obviously drive future organisational health, for example, a strong talent pipeline and impactful training. All these activities support one other: strong managers drive down the number of disputes and also retain and develop talent.

Capturing HR's purpose into measures that are owned across the organisation ensures that they get the attention they deserve.

Those HR leaders who use data proficiently and persuasively to make a business case are highly regarded. Some HR outcomes are difficult to measure with hard data. It's better to measure something that matters with soft data than not at all. If you're credible, people listen.

What vision do stakeholders have for HR?

Consider your stakeholder map from Chapter 5, about **Connection**. You identified those with whom you needed to engage. Let's now look at this from their perspective – how many of them would put *you* on *their* stakeholder map? How much have they thought about what HR could do for them? So, first, you need to be on their radar.

Then, at every level, HR needs to fully understand what success looks like for its key stakeholders. This is a revealing question to ask, and leaders enjoy answering it. It opens up areas for common ground – actually, we know that we all want the same outcomes, we just see them differently. This question enables us to find the right language to make our case, and work with the goals we share.

What does success look like for you? This big, fat question helps us, as the enquirer, to take a big step up. It's so open that it encourages the stakeholder to go into a different part of their intellect from the everyday. The step up is taken not just in the level of the conversation, but also in how we are perceived. We are judged by the quality of our questions.

Think of a key stakeholder with whom you would like to raise the level of your interactions. It can be less challenging to start with someone's area or function, for example, "What would success look like for your team?" Then, it's more comfortable to follow on by asking what success would look like for them, personally. It's often that second level of questioning which reveals how you can move your relationship up a level.

It is politically intelligent to do this proactively: to find out what is important for them and explain what is important to you. You build a strong foundation for robust and creative discussion.

How do you explore the future with stakeholders?

Stepping up as the HR function, together, requires many conversations across the organisation about the future. Powerful, open questions enable you both to explore the future. You can then build the picture using data, anecdotes and examples.

The purpose of exploring the future is to be able to anticipate as accurately as possible. As we know, most measures are retrospective – they tell us only about the past. To anticipate our capabilities to meet future challenges is less of a science and more of an art, where we deploy our experience and intuition. We can look at trends and patterns in our data, our sector, market or community and the wider world, but these are tools to assist the human brain. The most successful businesspeople do not follow the path most trodden; they take a leap of faith.

Having said that, research tells us that business leaders want HR to become masters of data. Data forms a solid foundation of fact from which to explore. It also enables HR to make clear links between HR activities and business outcomes. Being sufficiently savvy with data to make predictions about HR outcomes is a very neat trick and a major step up.

There is no one right way to put your strategy on to paper; I have seen it done in many different ways that reflect the organisation's unique character and in-house styles and methodologies. Naturally, it will always start with the business goals and priorities and relate all HR activities to those.

For my part, I developed a simple way to check the relevance of our HR activities. It's so simple that it doesn't necessarily work as a strategic document to share with others, rather as a method to cross-check and challenge the targeting of your HR strategy. This has helped me to build a cohesive strategy and manage my limited resources.

First, clarify the top business priorities. Here, for the sake of offering an example, I am using three priorities that apply to most organisations:

1. Growth in revenue, income or however you measure how much you are doing of what you do.

2. Profit or margin, that is, how cost-effectively you are doing it.

3. Growth in skills or talent, or learning, that is, the development of people.

Second, consider the key tools, specialisms or workstreams that you have in HR and put those along the other axis. Here I have used some typical areas, but this list is not exclusive:

	Growth	Profit	People development
Reward	Reward sales...	...at the right margin	
Resourcing	Workforce planning anticipates demand	...and avoids costs of redundancies	Right skills, right place, right time
Management development	Tailored programme drives alignment	Optimal use of virtual resources	
Succession planning	Retains talent with visible career path; continuity in CRM	Reduces hassle, costs of recruitment, onboarding, training	Provides development opportunities

The third, and final stage, is to test how each workstream specifically relates to each business goal and contributes actively to its achievement. I have made some suggestions above, which can be made much more relevant and impactful when they relate to a particular organisation and your projects. I'll leave you to fill in the gaps and make this specific to your organisation.

How do you make sure strategic interventions deliver results?

Here we have another opportunity to drive collaboration between HR and the line. Often interventions are designed by the centres of expertise, and one risk is that distance can develop between the experts and the front line. Where an organisation has that structure, is likely also to have the HR business partner to bridge the gap. Use that relationship to ensure that front-line realities are respected in the solution, and that you also get the benefit of best practice expertise.

Whatever the structure or roles in your organisation, you can drive the effectiveness and impact of HR interventions from the top. First, engage in collaboration to ensure that the design truly responds to real needs. Second, drive the partnership from the top, at every level that will ensure its successful delivery.

How can we achieve co-creation with our stakeholders?

Let's focus now on the top right-hand box of my business partnering matrix. When we assemble intelligent people, who have great expertise, insight and wisdom, wonderful things can happen that could not otherwise have been conceived.

While working for a large, global organisation, I had the opportunity to go to its global research centre. It was the perfect venue for our session with its high-potential HR leaders from around the world. We kicked off with a presentation from the research director there who told us a little about how they generated innovation. He said, "The greatest innovation comes from the intersection of two disciplines." He illustrated this with a story about taking experts from two scientific disciplines, without any apparent overlap, and quite simply putting them in a room together. A microbiologist and a microphysicist came up with the idea of using human X-ray technology to find tiny faults in aircraft wings. They both worked at the molecular level; that was their common ground, and they went from there.

How can organisations create the conditions for that kind of co-creation? Answering that question could fill another book, and would include building trust, psychological safety, and mastery, as well as removing blocks such as resources or fear of failure. If we focus in on co-creation between HR leaders and their fellow leaders, we can identify two important areas to explore.

These in fact reflect our axes on the business partnering matrix:

1. What do we each need to learn about the other's area to be able to build from there?

2. What do we need to understand about the future that we want to build?

This helps us identify what we can work on, and why it's important. We are assuming that the two people can get on well enough with each other to spark the debate, and we have taken out of the equation the inherent conflicts that, in reality, may get in the way.

Making this work, whatever it takes, is key to ensuring that HR interventions are seen through to full implementation. This is where you get maximum return from the investment – no wasted seats on training programmes; no wasted time with people arguing about performance ratings; no key talent leaving because their career path wasn't made clear by their manager.

Most often, less is more. Taking time, and using creativity, to make things as simple as possible pays dividends. Most people, at every level, are busy and need HR to do the work to make things easy for them to digest, understand, engage with, sell to others and implement. Creating an appetite for interventions enables HR to be seen to be meeting a real need rather than creating more work.

Wouldn't it be useful to think of it as less of a 'roll-out' and more of a 'pull-in'? When the collaboration drives a design that fits effortlessly into the organisation, and therefore sticks, it is so much easier to create energetic partnerships at every level of implementation.

Stepping up as a function demands this level of challenge, creativity and openness to exploration. This works only where you have first established a thorough understanding of what really matters in your organisation, and how it works.

And finally - celebrate HR's achievements

Along the journey, capture HR's story of learning, exploration and achievement, and add this to your strategic narrative, "This is what we learned, this is how we responded and engaged, how we co-created and came up with such a great solution, and here's what we have achieved together, with our fellow leaders and managers." Endings are important, and often we quite simply forget to tie up the threads into a neat celebration.

Building up all the dimensions of the measures at HR's disposal is vital to ensure that its credibility is further enhanced by success. Whether it's reminding leaders about how smoothly HR is running things, or the results of more visible interventions, this data is crucial to driving HR's influence upwards.

Be proud of HR's story. It's good for everyone in the organisation, and in the world of work, when HR is valued.

What next?

These are exciting times to be involved in driving the people agenda. Great HR has never been more important. In writing this book, my aim is to enhance the influence, credibility and confidence of HR.

Please connect and engage on LinkedIn so that we can continue to share and debate what great HR looks like and celebrate successes.

https://www.linkedin.com/in/deborahwilkes/

Resources

a. **Resources on transactional analysis**

 a) *Games People Play* by Eric Berne is the original.

 b) *Born to Win* by Muriel James and Dorothy Jongeward is an inspiring book used by psychotherapists.

b. **Business partnering**
https://www.linkedin.com/pulse/human-resources-hr-business-partner-20-dave-ulrich/

c. **HR scorecard**

 a) *The HR Scorecard* by Dave Ulrich, Brian E Becker and Mark A Huselid: Harvard Business Review Press.

 b) Dave Ulrich also offers a framework to audit your HR function: https://www.linkedin.com/pulse/effectiveness-audit-your-hr-department-dave-ulrich/

d. **Neuroscience**

 a) *Neuropsychology for Coaches* by Paul Brown and Virginia Brown: McGraw Hill.

 b) *In an Unspoken Voice* by Peter A Levine, PhD: North Atlantic Books; for a longer read.

e. **Emotional intelligence**

 a) *Working with Emotional Intelligence* by Daniel Goleman:

Bloomsbury.

f. Other inspiration

a) *Invictus* poem by William Ernest Henley: https://poets.org/poem/invictus

b) Update from Dave Ulrich on progress made by HR over 30 years: "These are dramatic improvements in the overall competence for HR professionals."

   https://www.linkedin.com/pulse/have-hr-professionals-made-progress-30-year-evolution-dave-ulrich/

About the author

Deborah Wilkes FCIPD has been passionate about HR and its value since her early career establishing and leading UK and European HR functions. Then, as a consultant and coach for over 25 years, she developed leaders and managers in some of the world's leading organisations.

In 2016, she and George Naylor researched what makes great HR. They created a unique framework of seven enablers and an evaluation tool. As chief executive of Enable-HR International, Deborah helps the HR function to become more strategic and business savvy in its approach, activities and behaviours.

She lives in England, near Bath, with her family and enjoys gardening and wildlife.

https://www.linkedin.com/in/deborahwilkes/

https://www.enable-hr.com

Printed in Great Britain
by Amazon

58363831R00116